I0489201

## NOTE FROM THE PUBLISHER

Who would have thought that a coloring book would be so soothing to an adult??!!

Well you believe it because you purchased this book! Thank you!

Coloring the drawings in this adult coloring book allows you to relax, focus on transforming the black and white drawings into a beautiful art pieces. Remember there is no right or wrong to this.

As you will notice there is a blank page after each drawing. This makes it easy for you to pull out the page from the book and stick it on your wall or maybe the door of your fridge! Also this eliminates the issue of the coloring of the previous drawings to be visible on the other page.

Enjoy!

www.book-o-rama.com

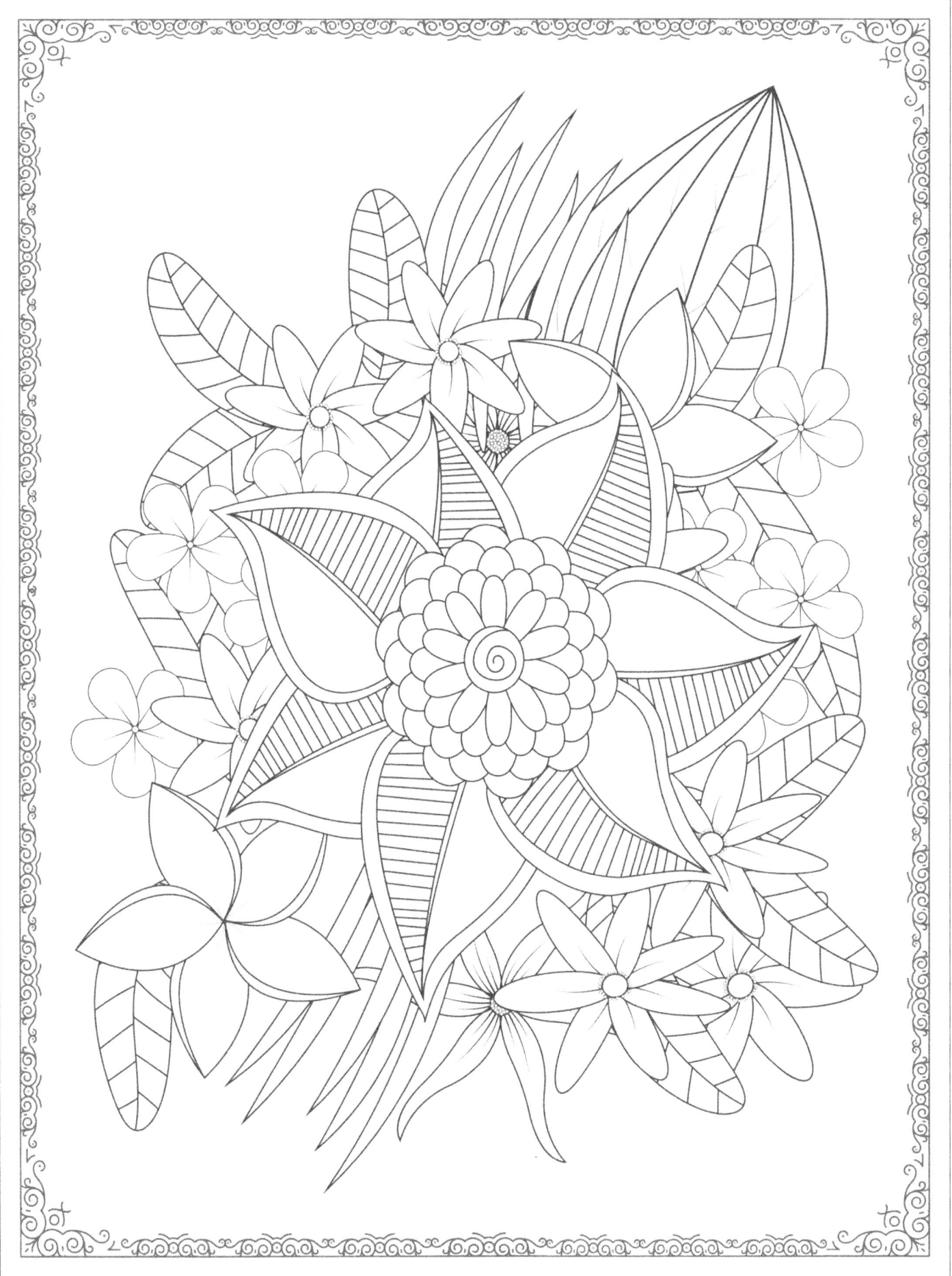

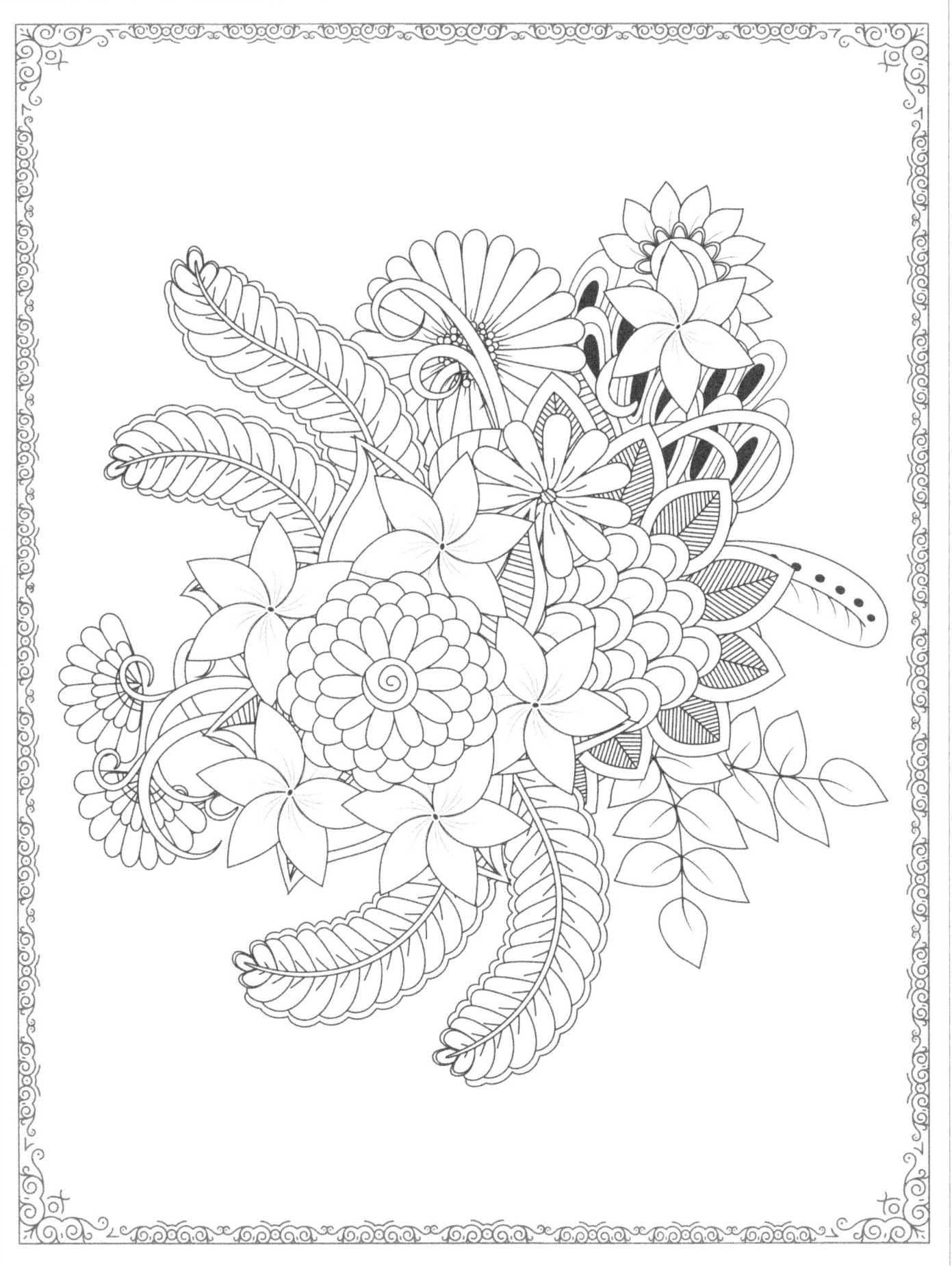

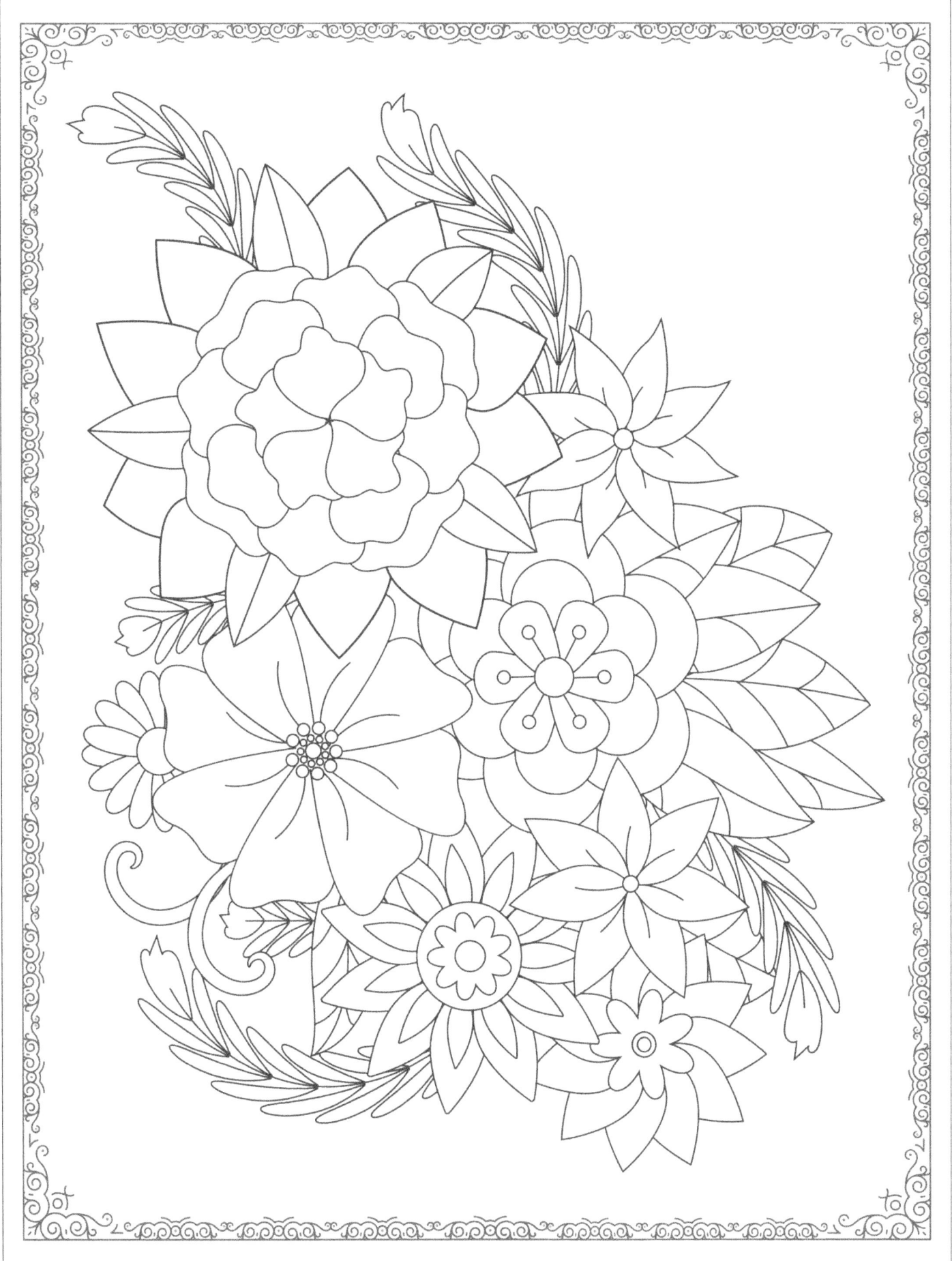

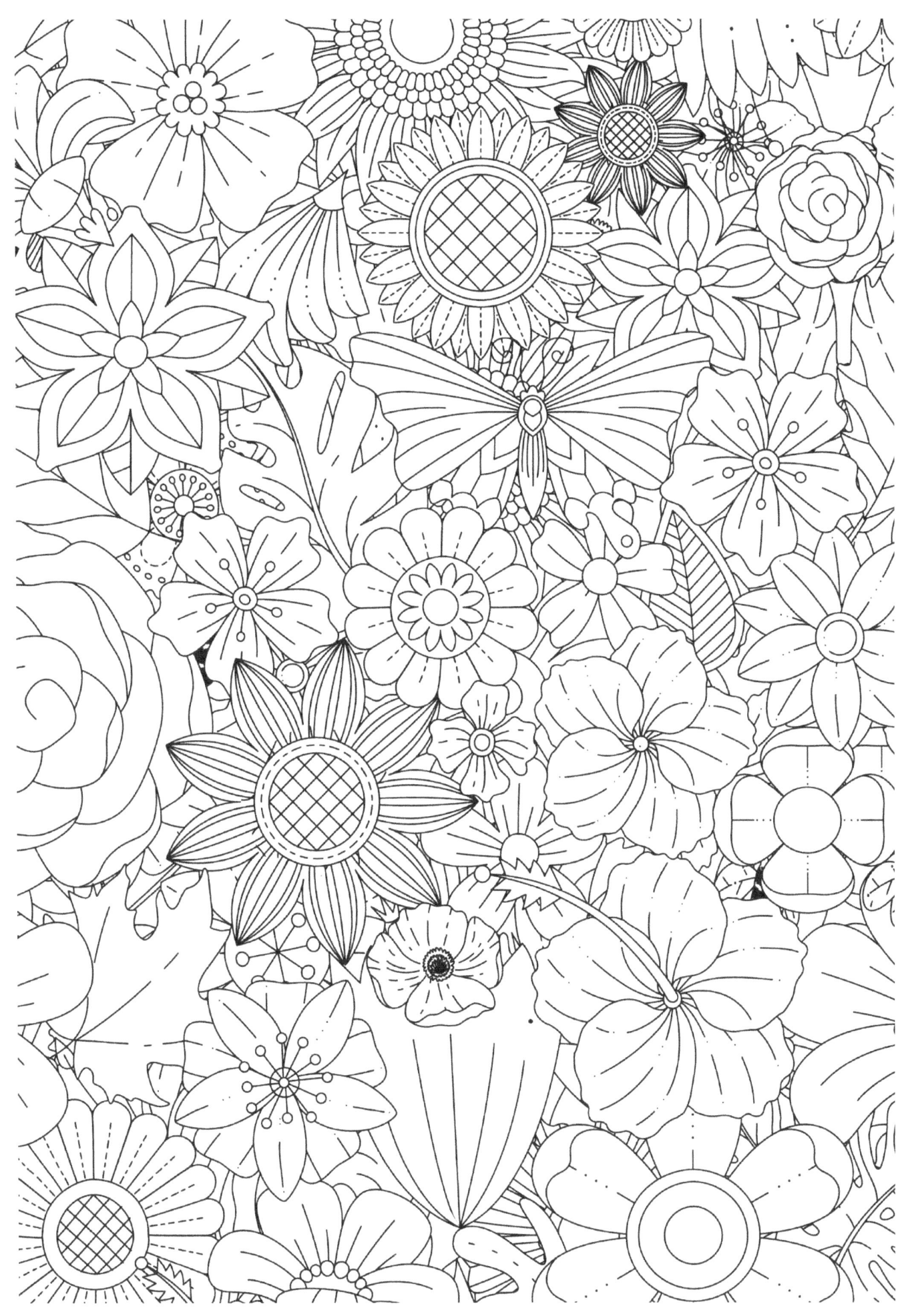

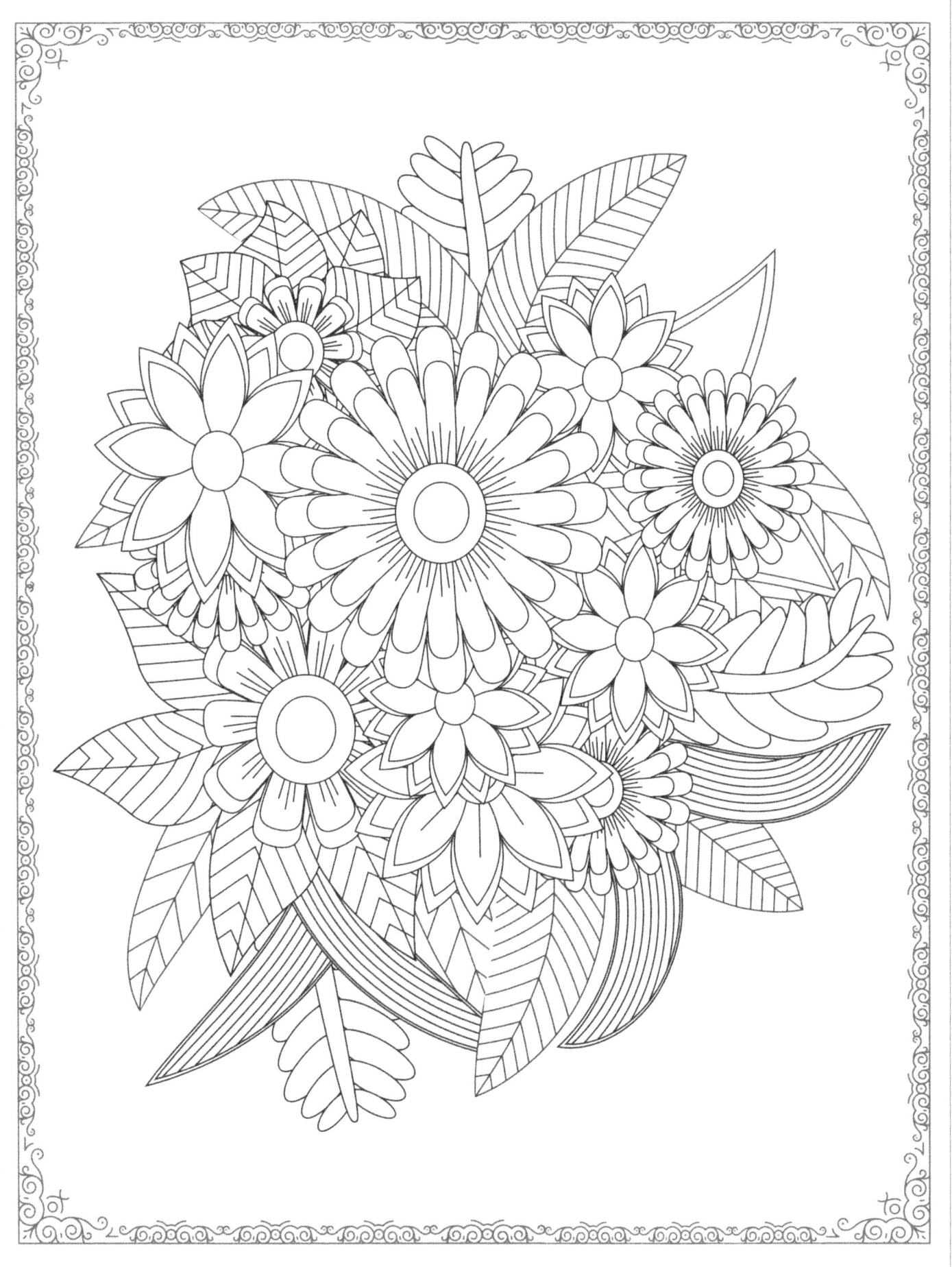

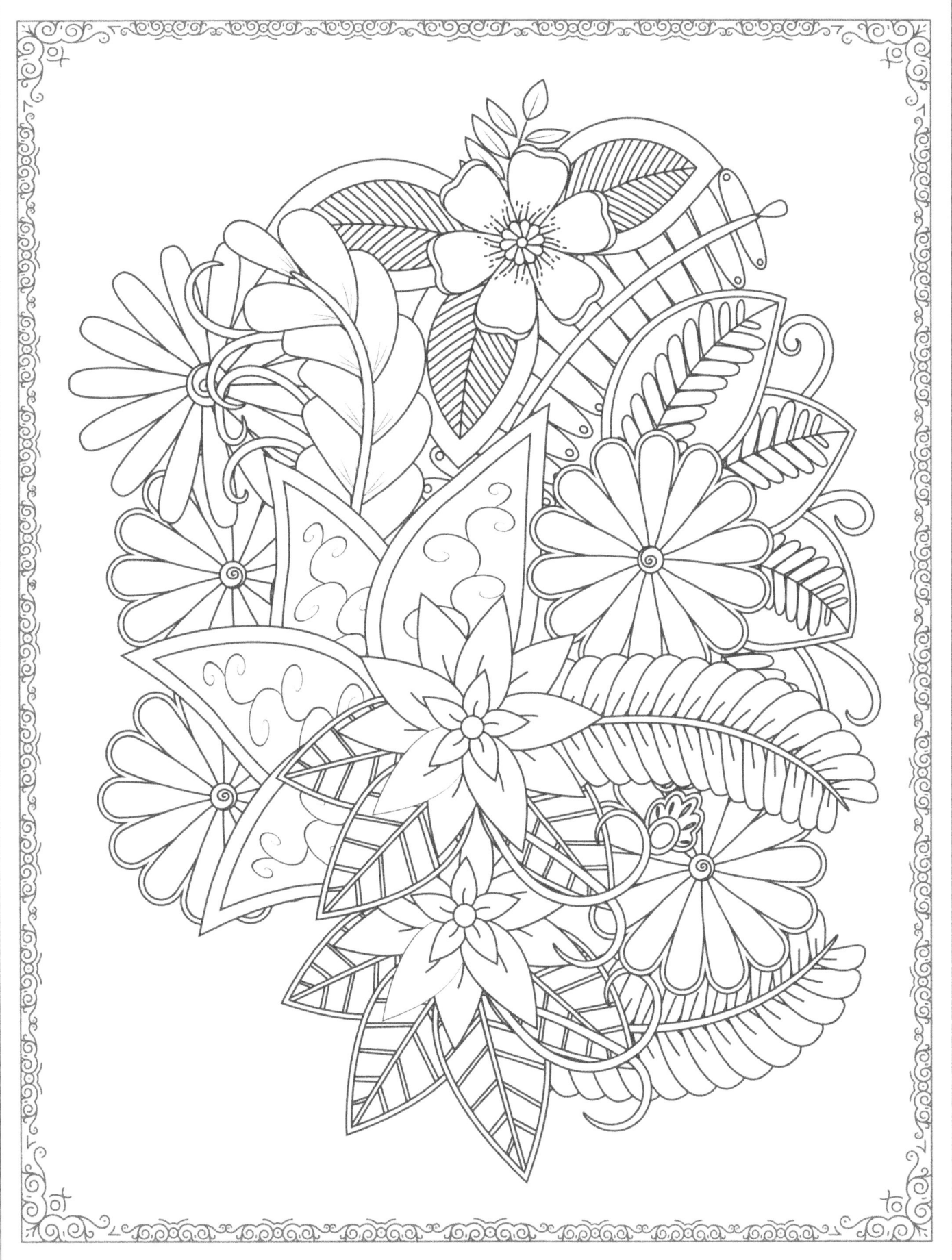

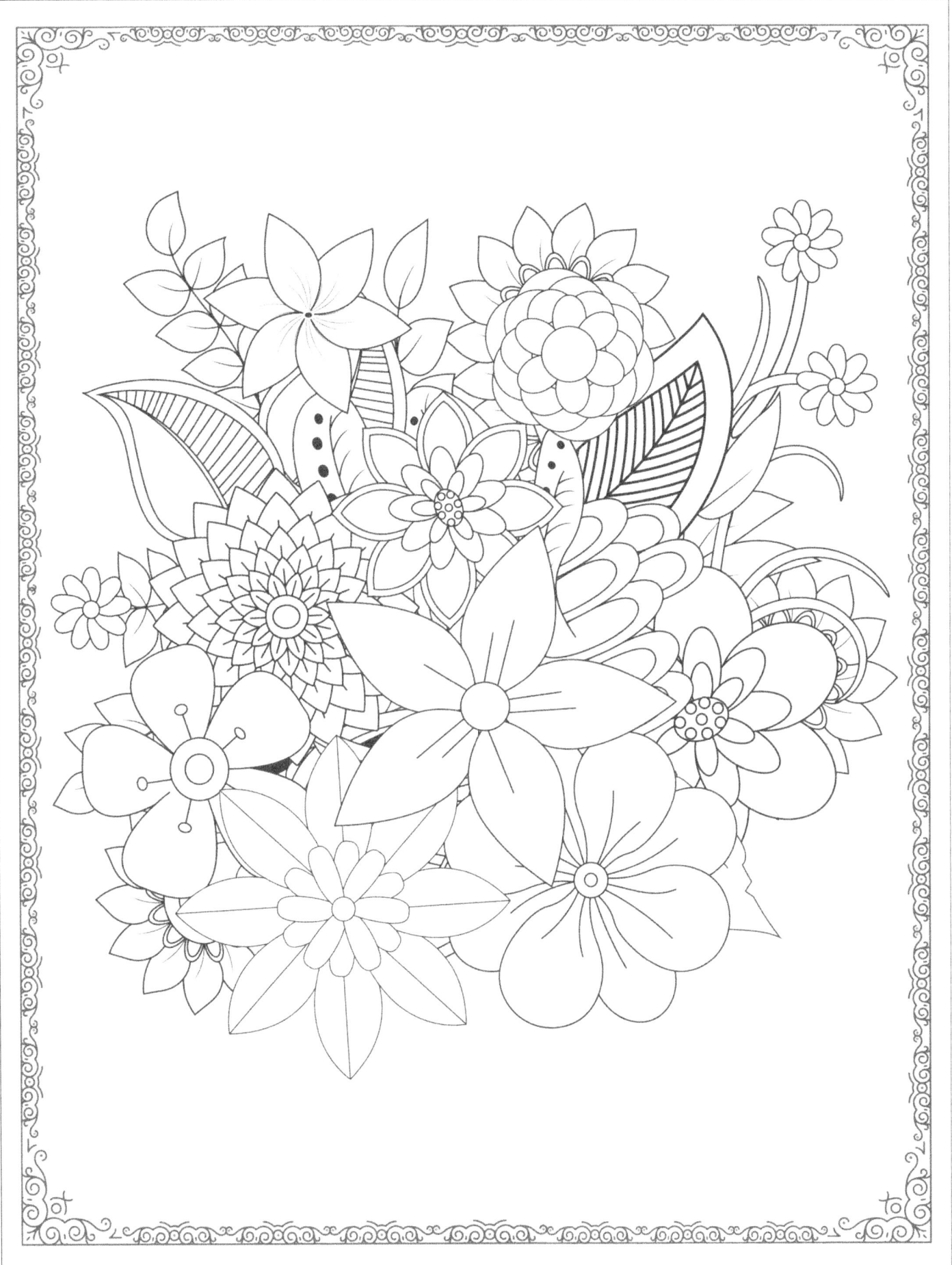

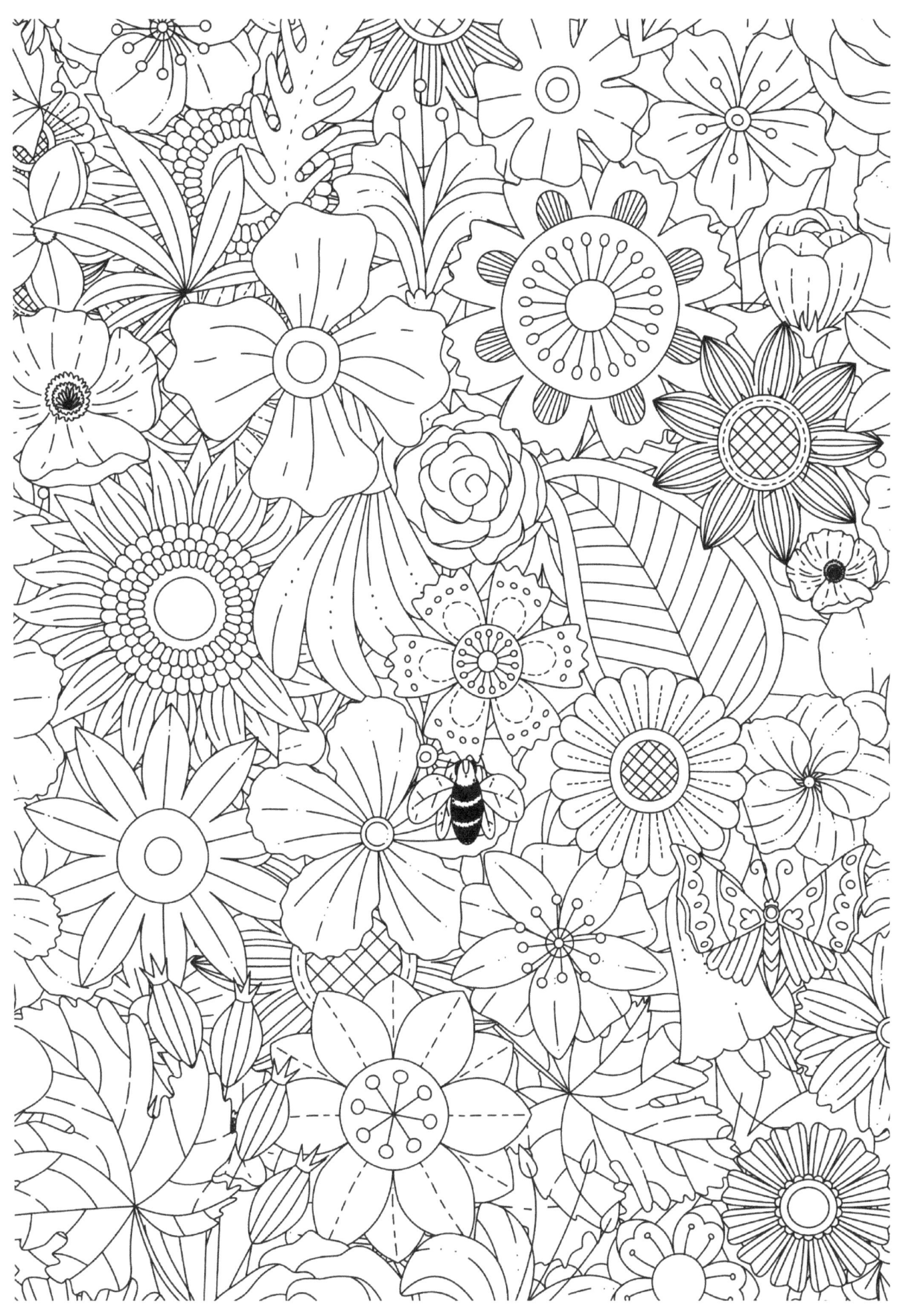

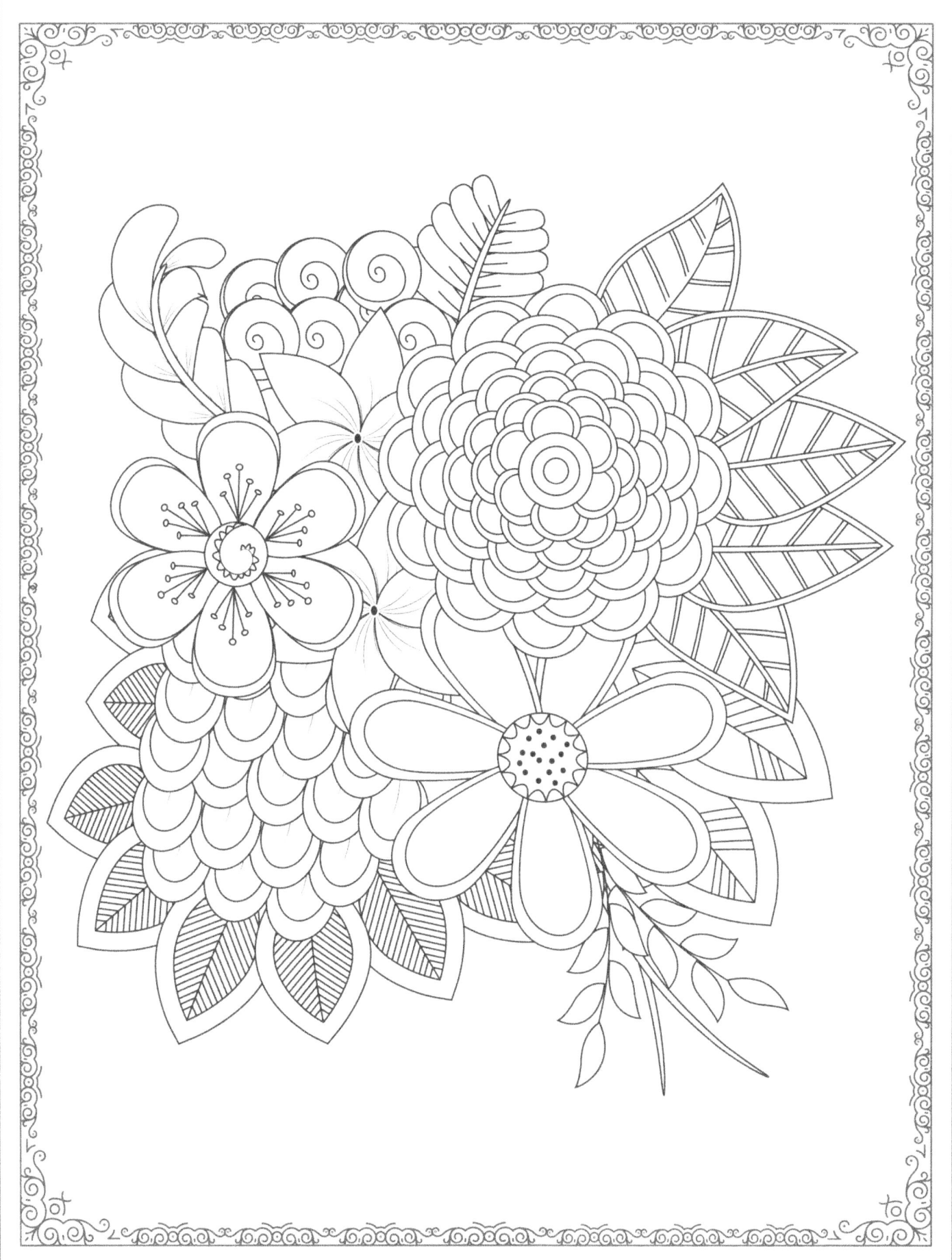

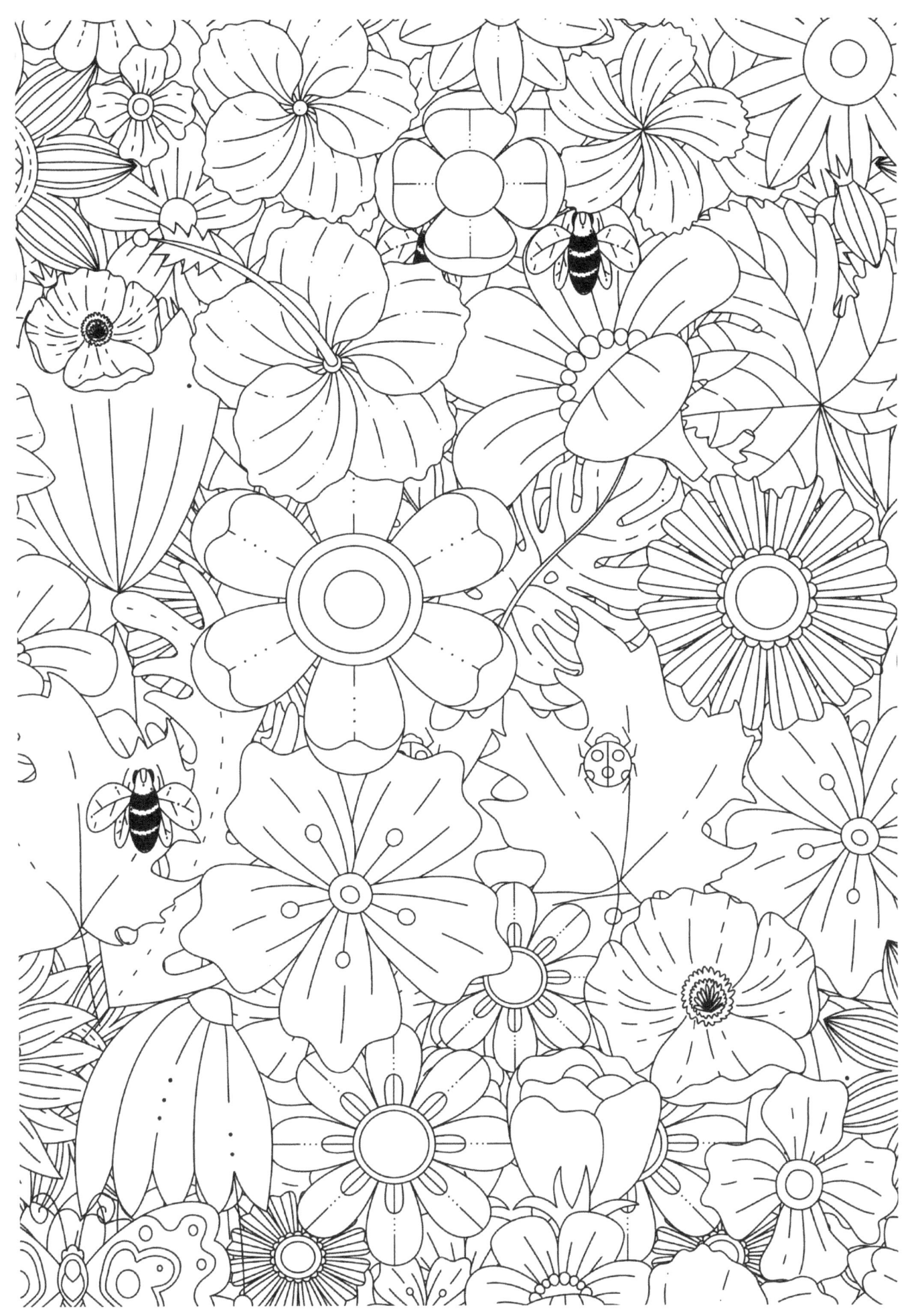

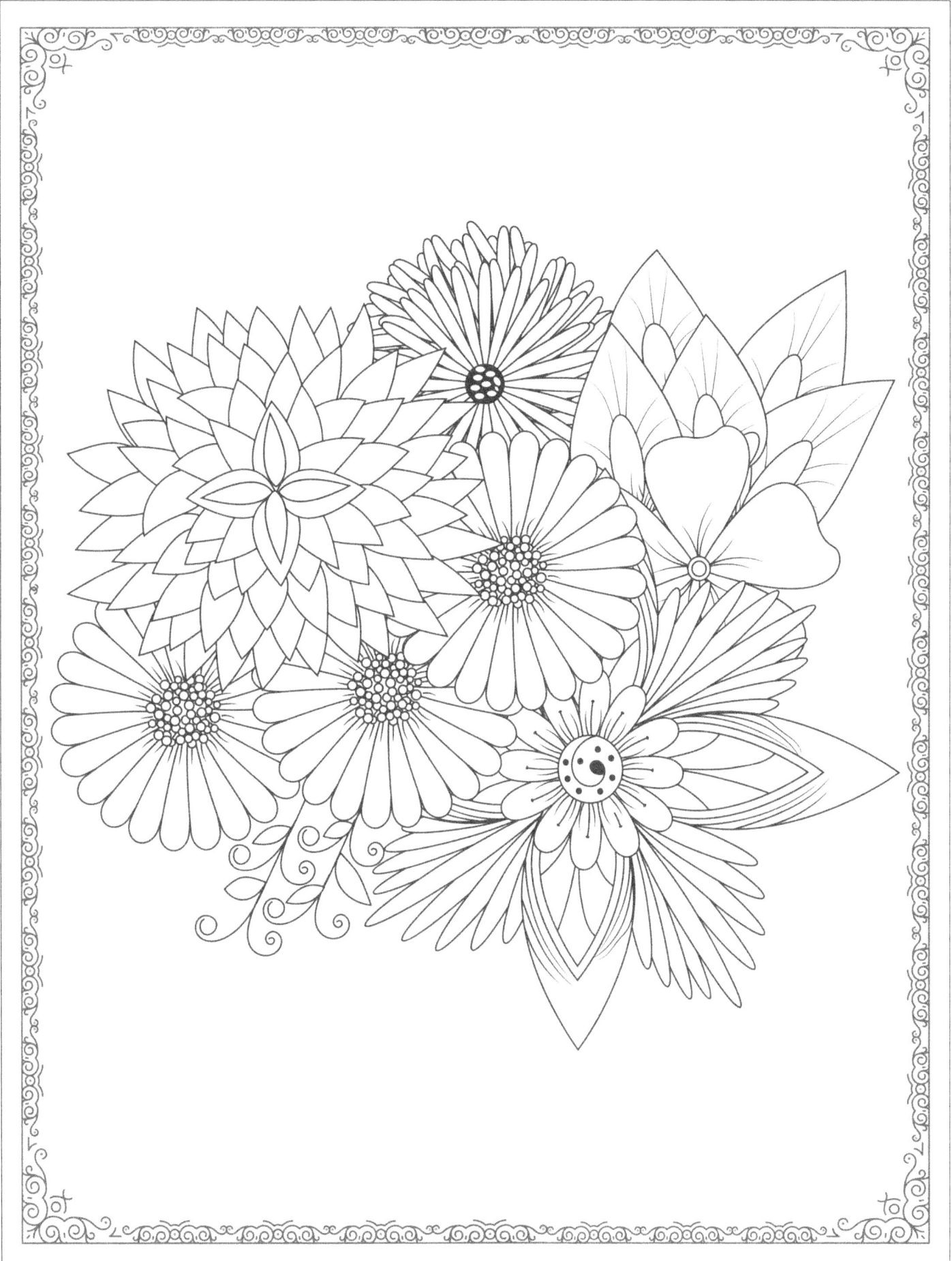

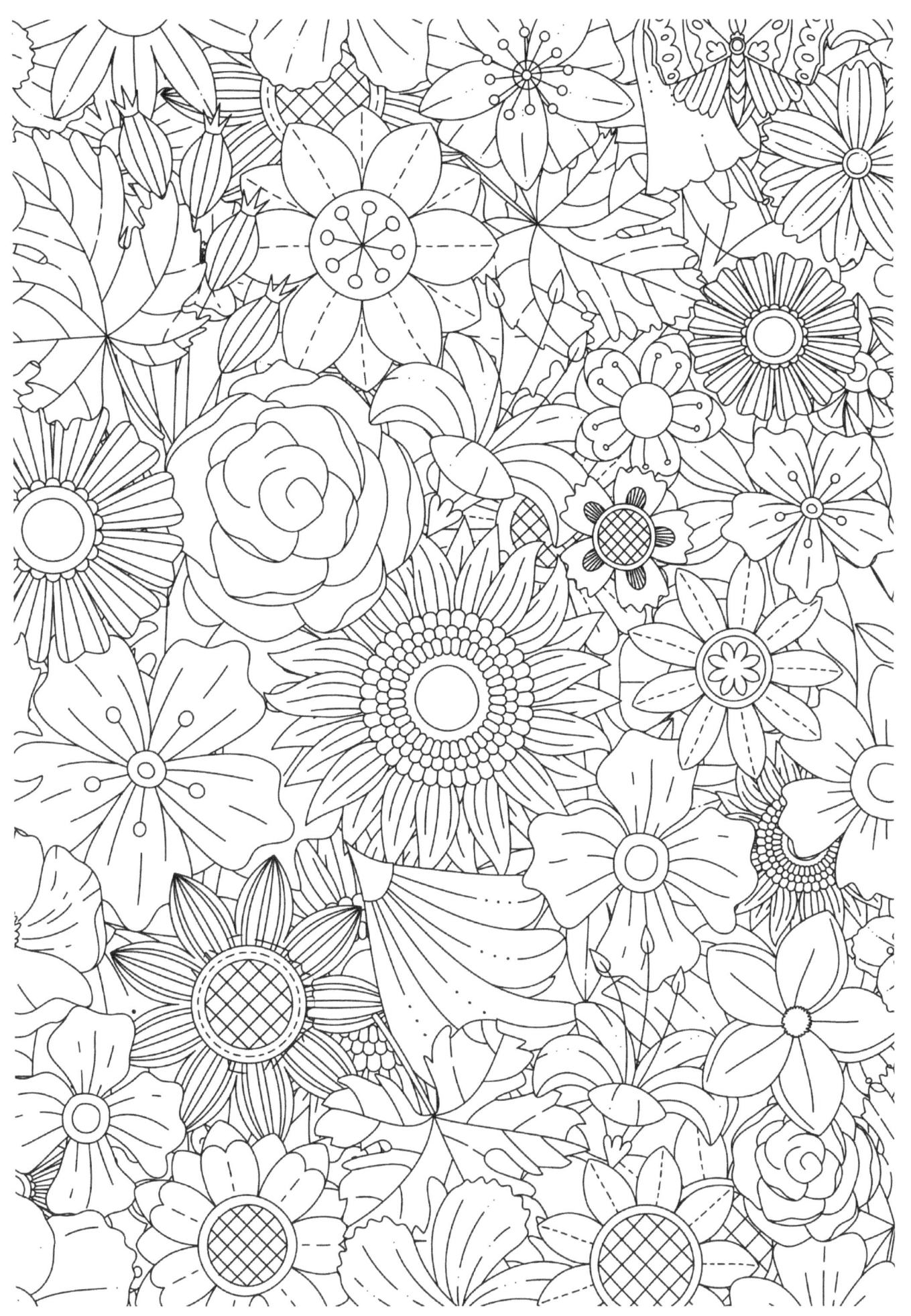

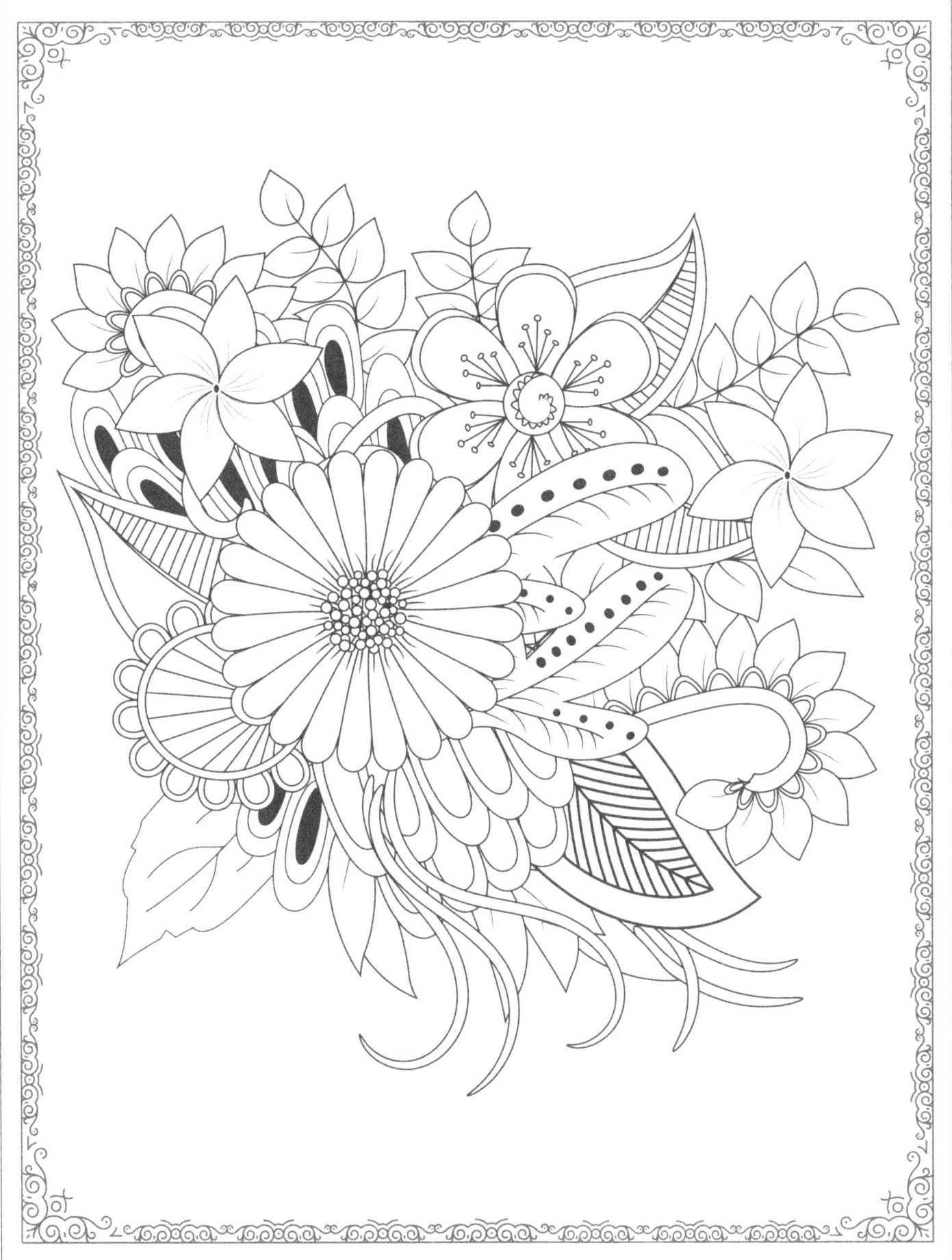

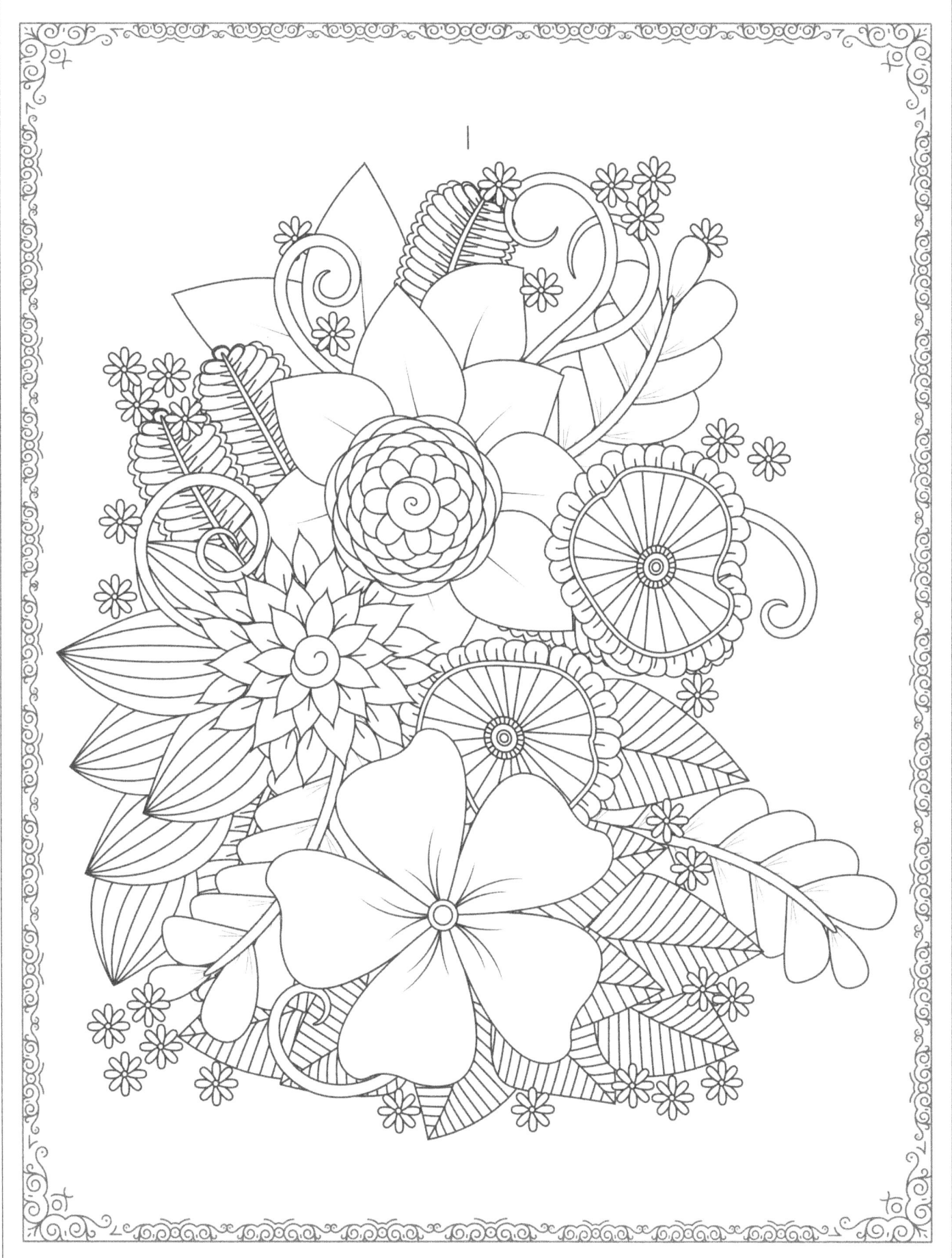

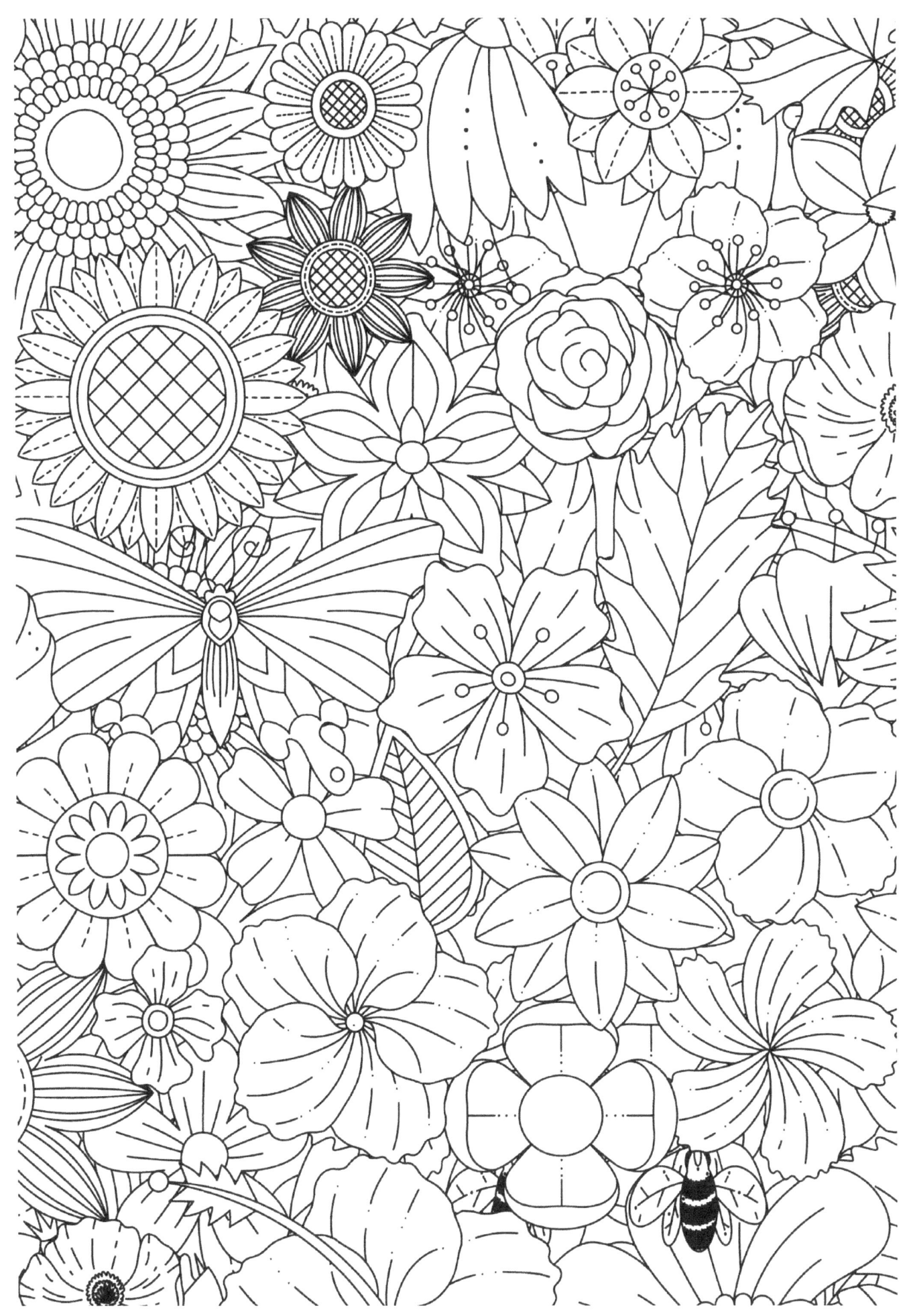

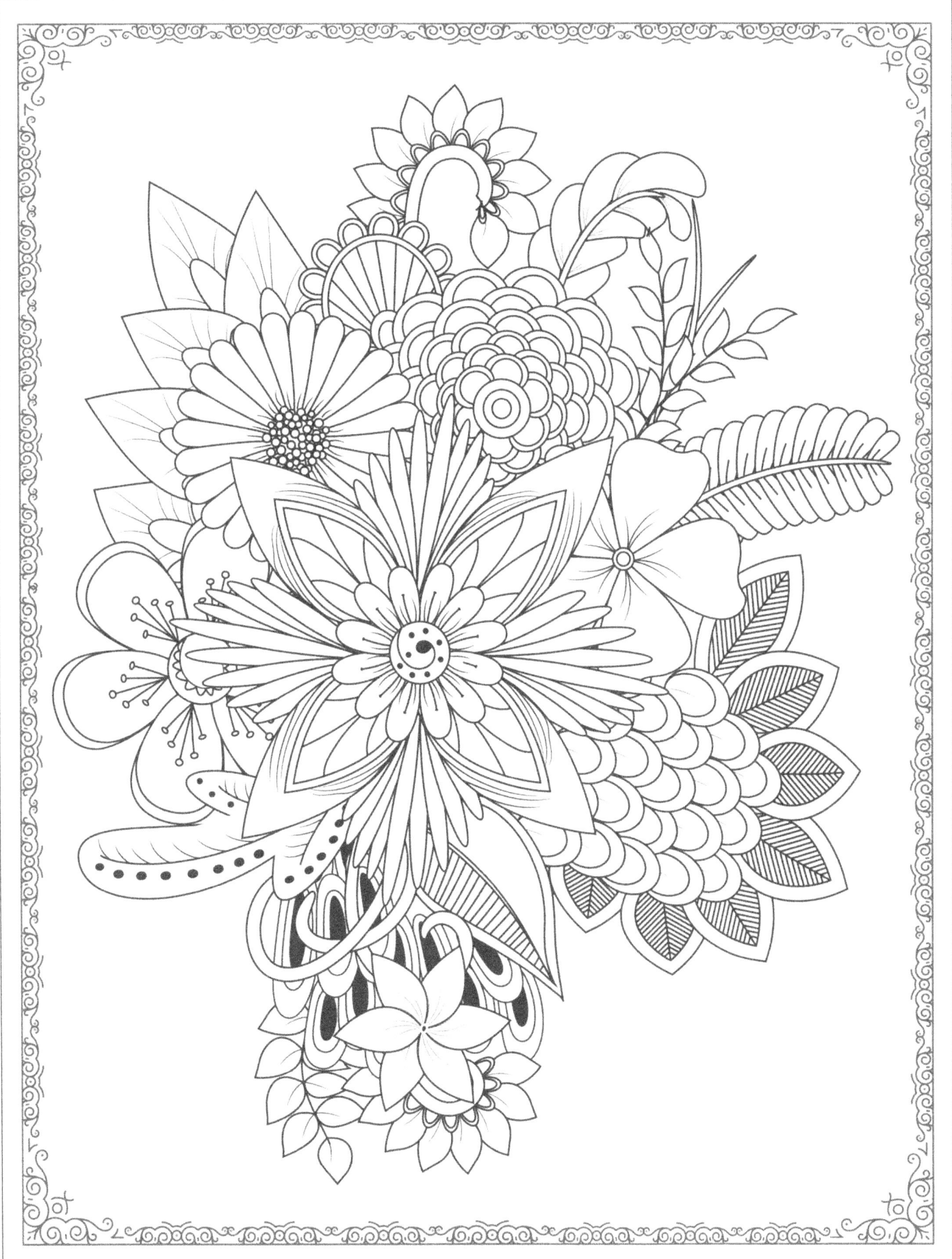

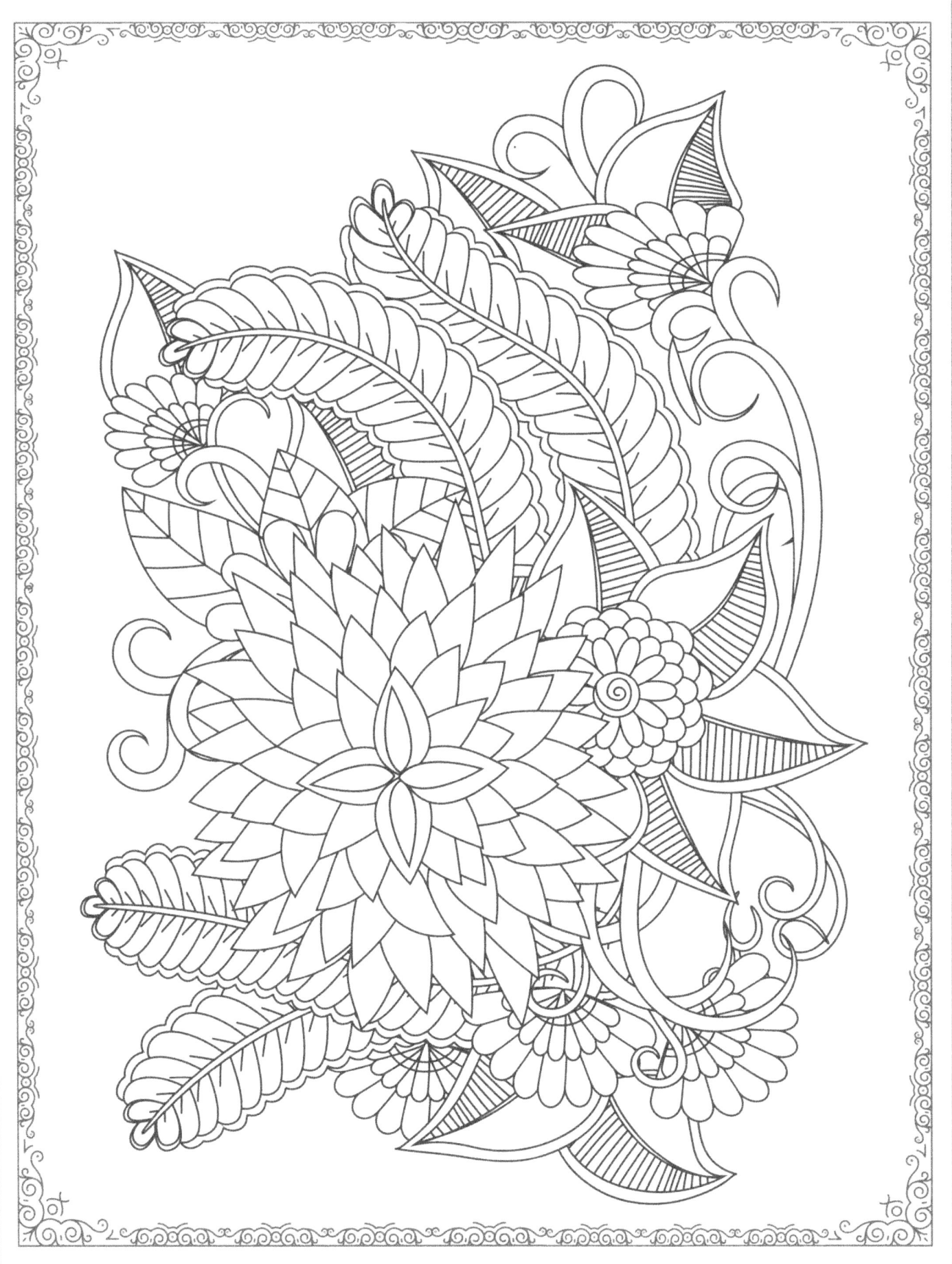

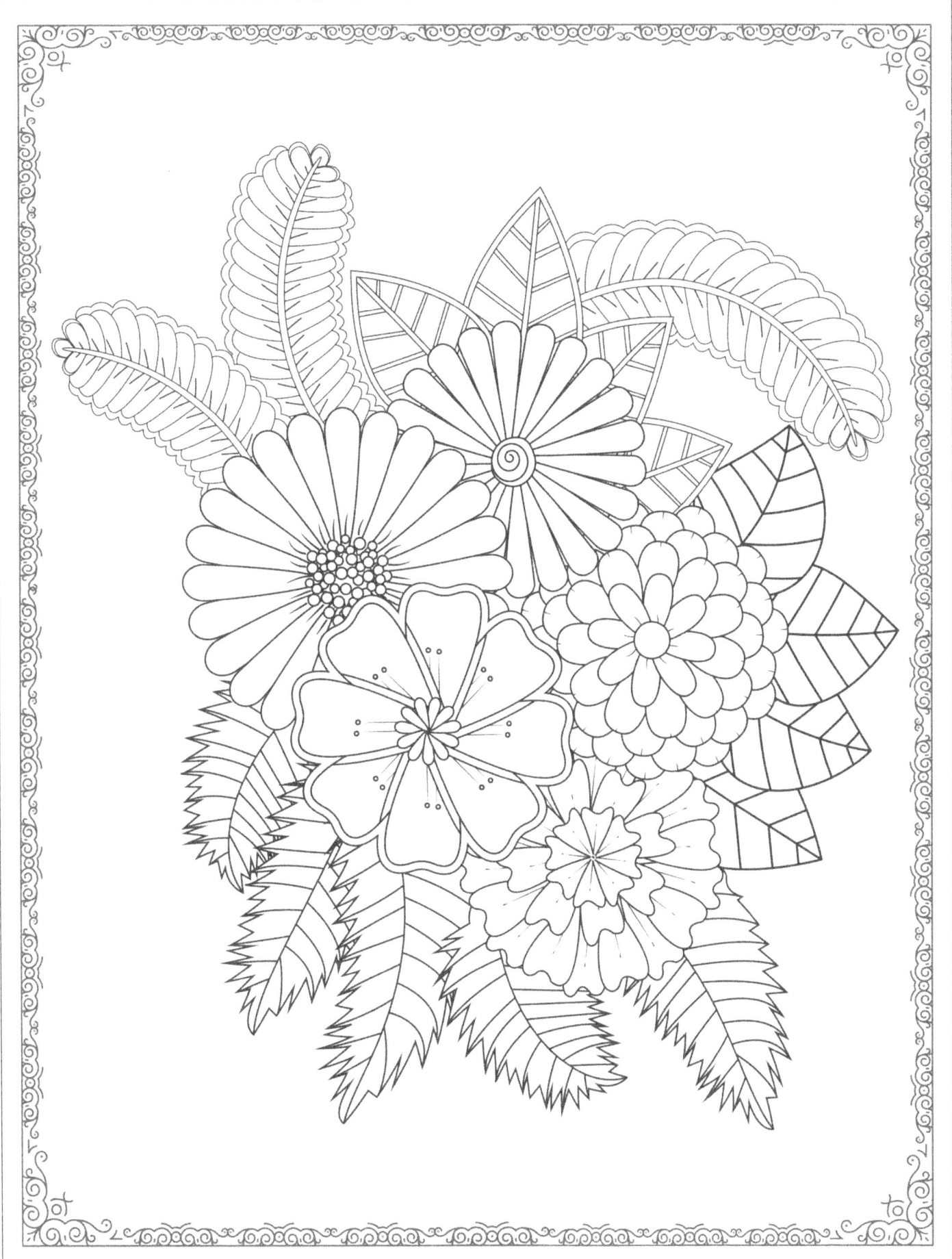

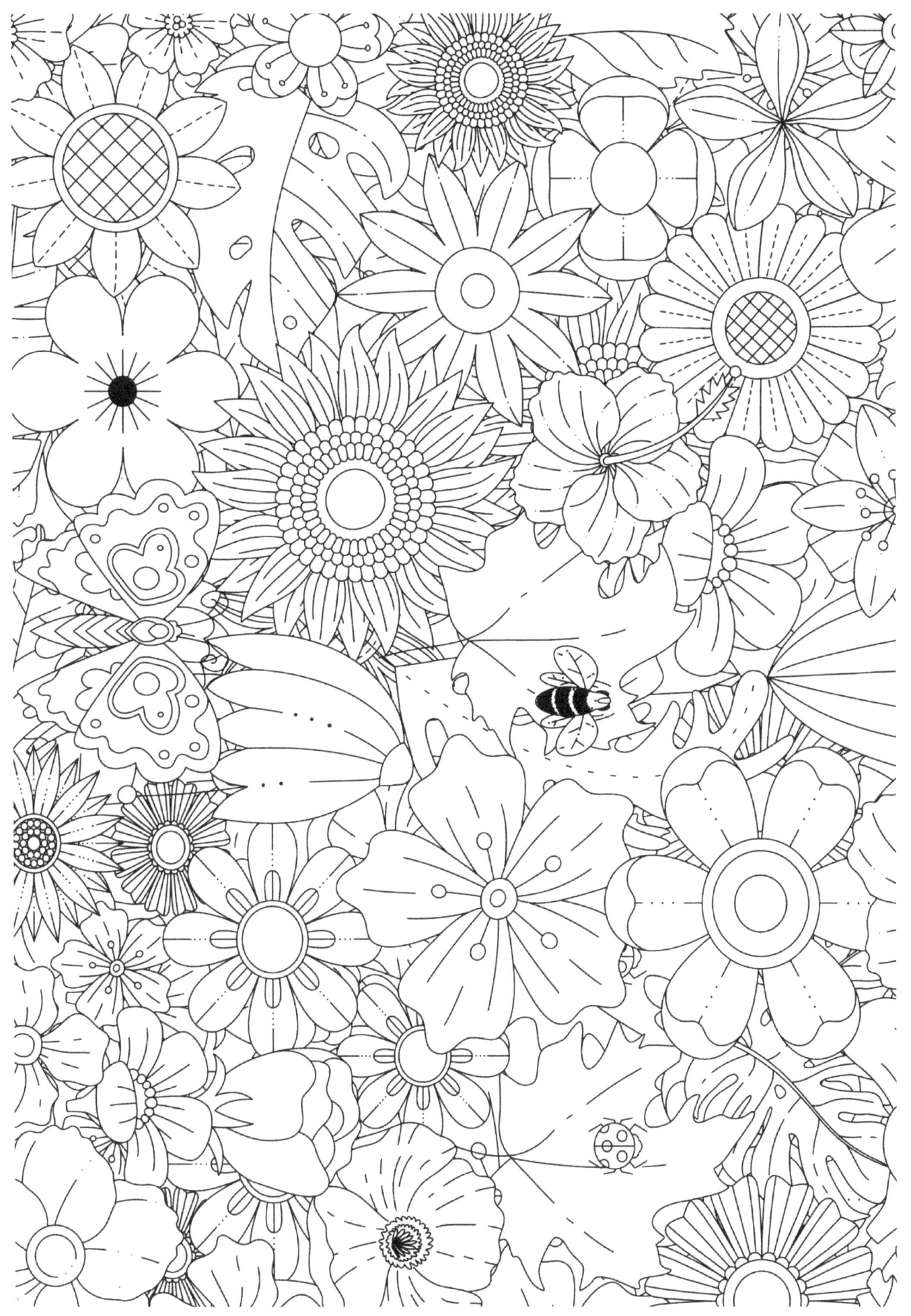

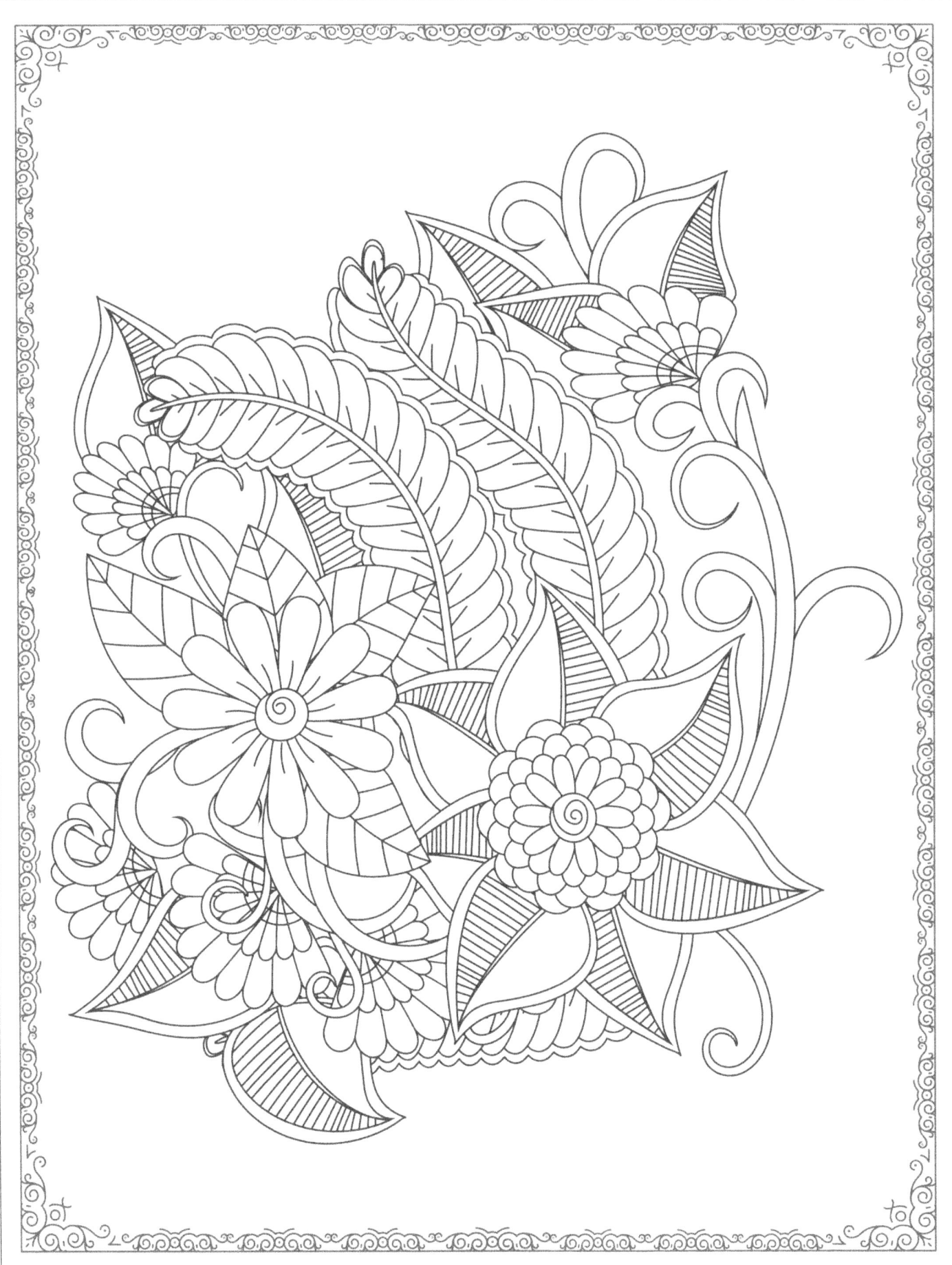

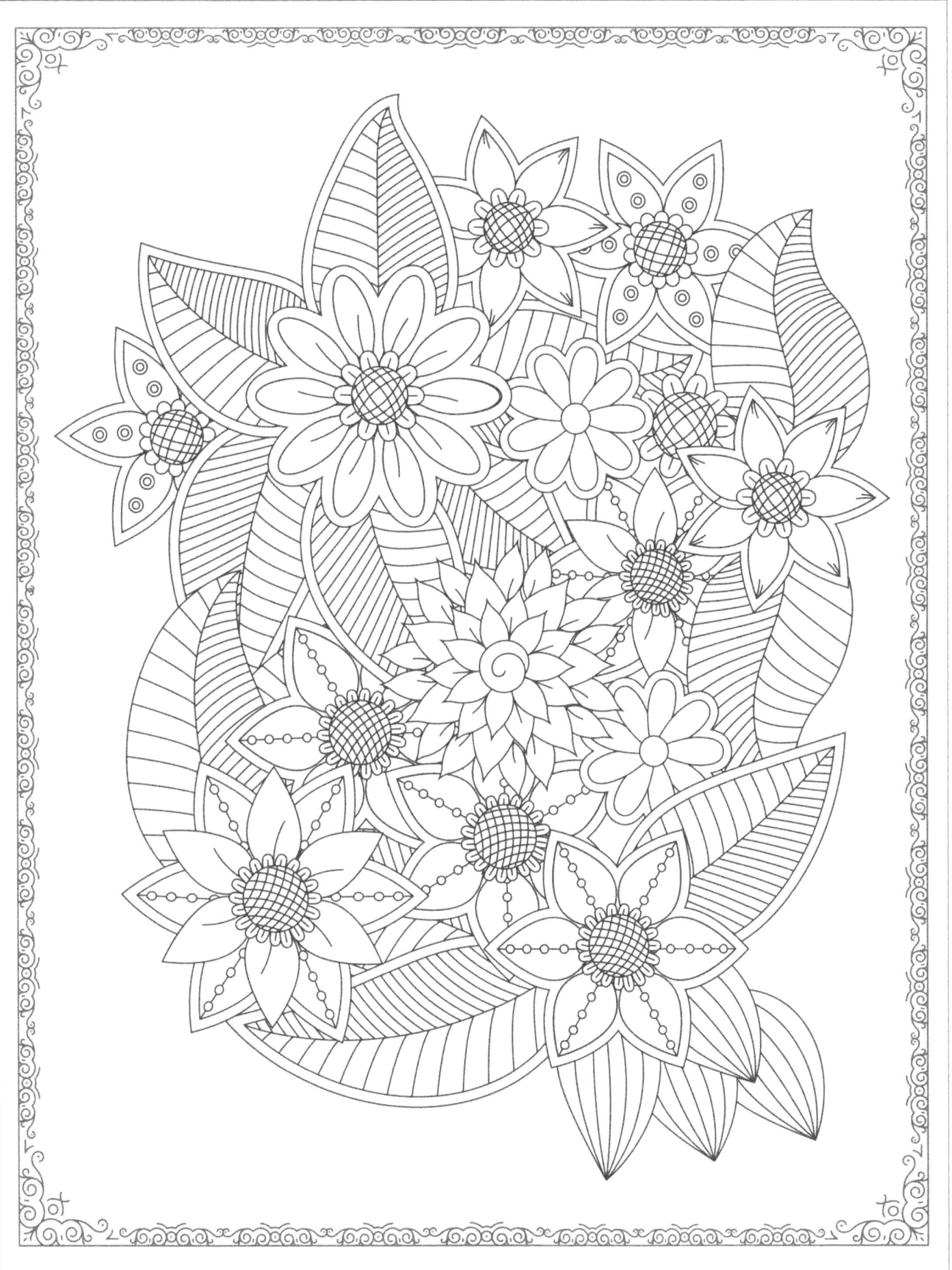

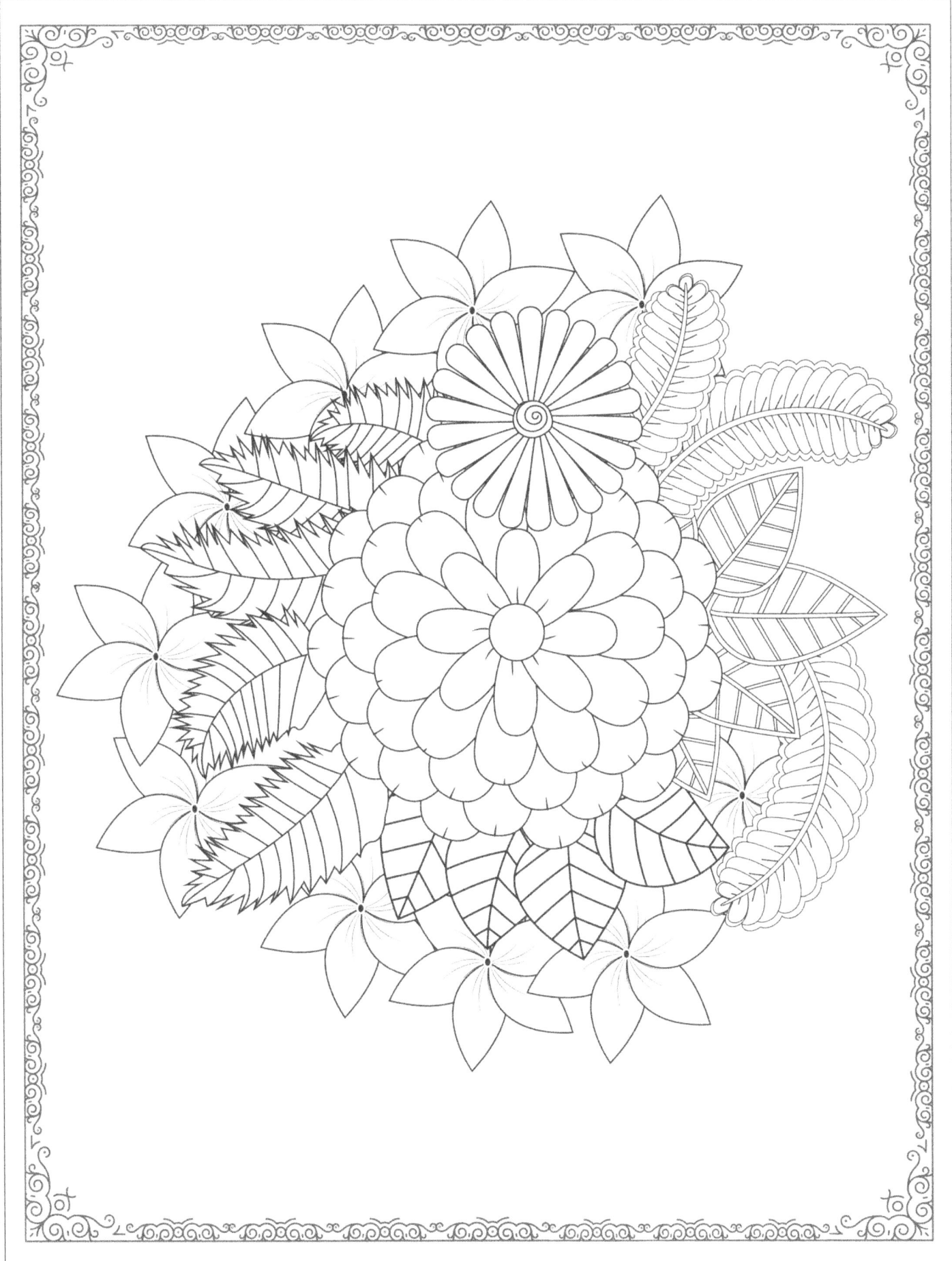

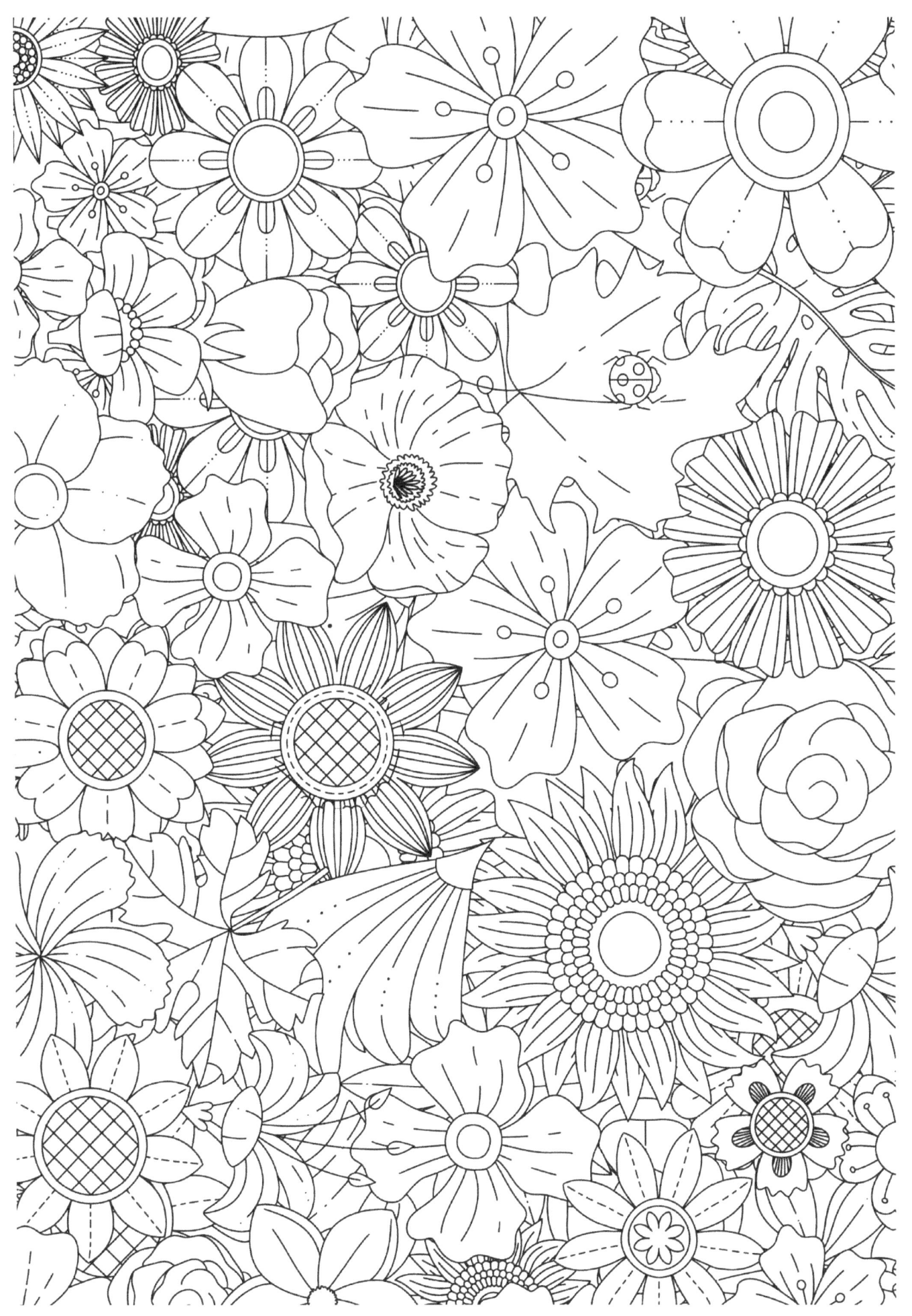

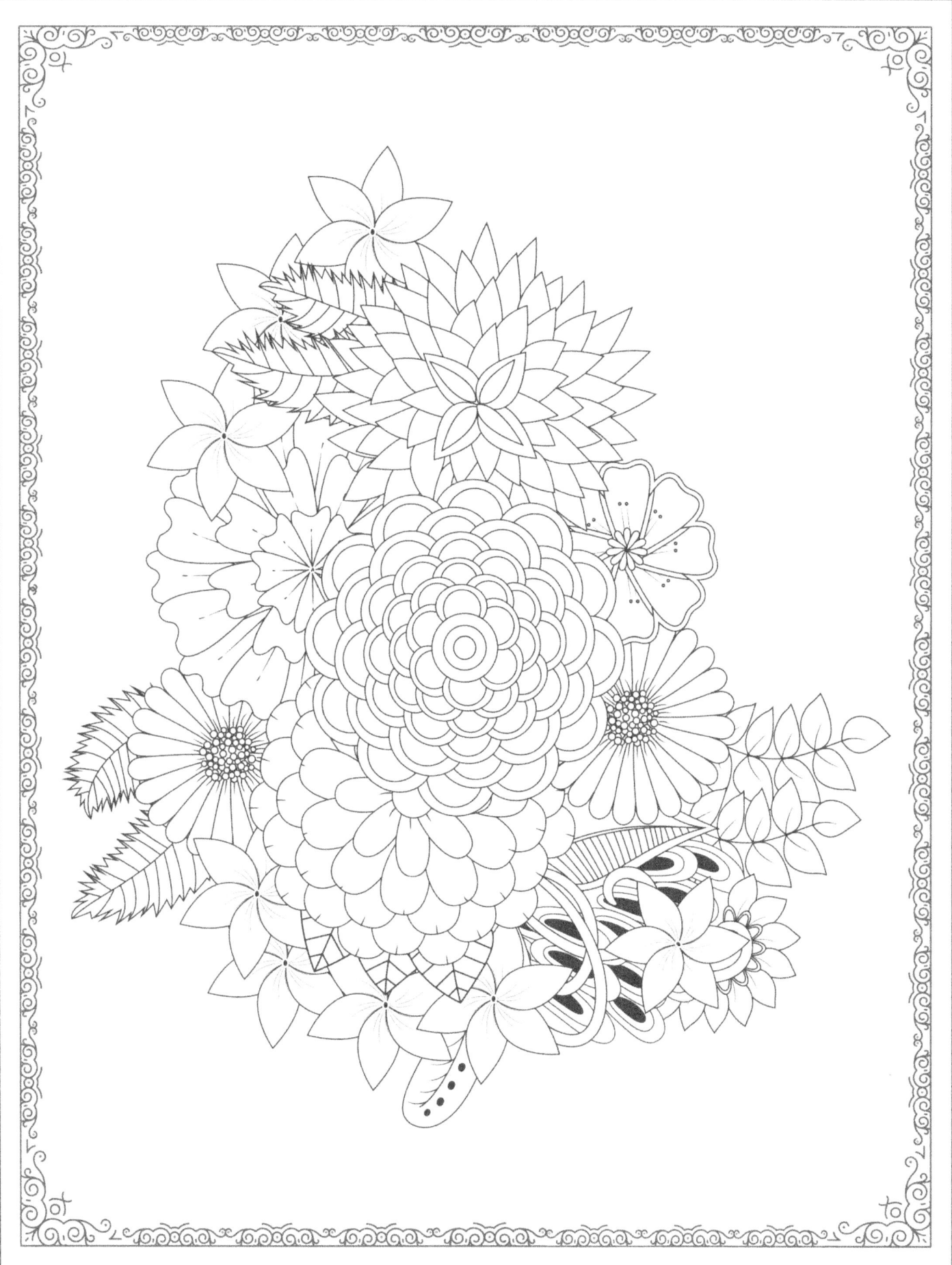

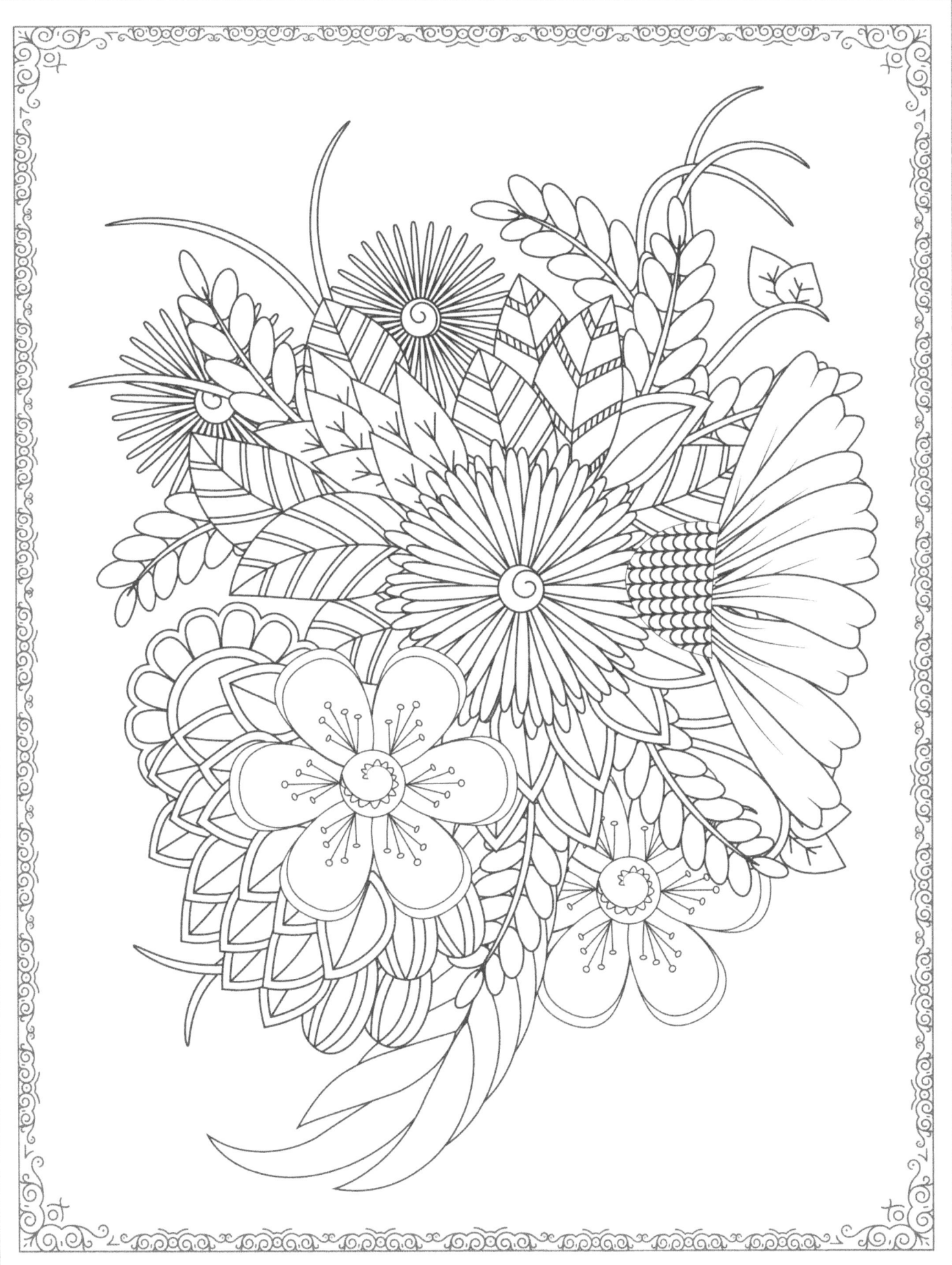

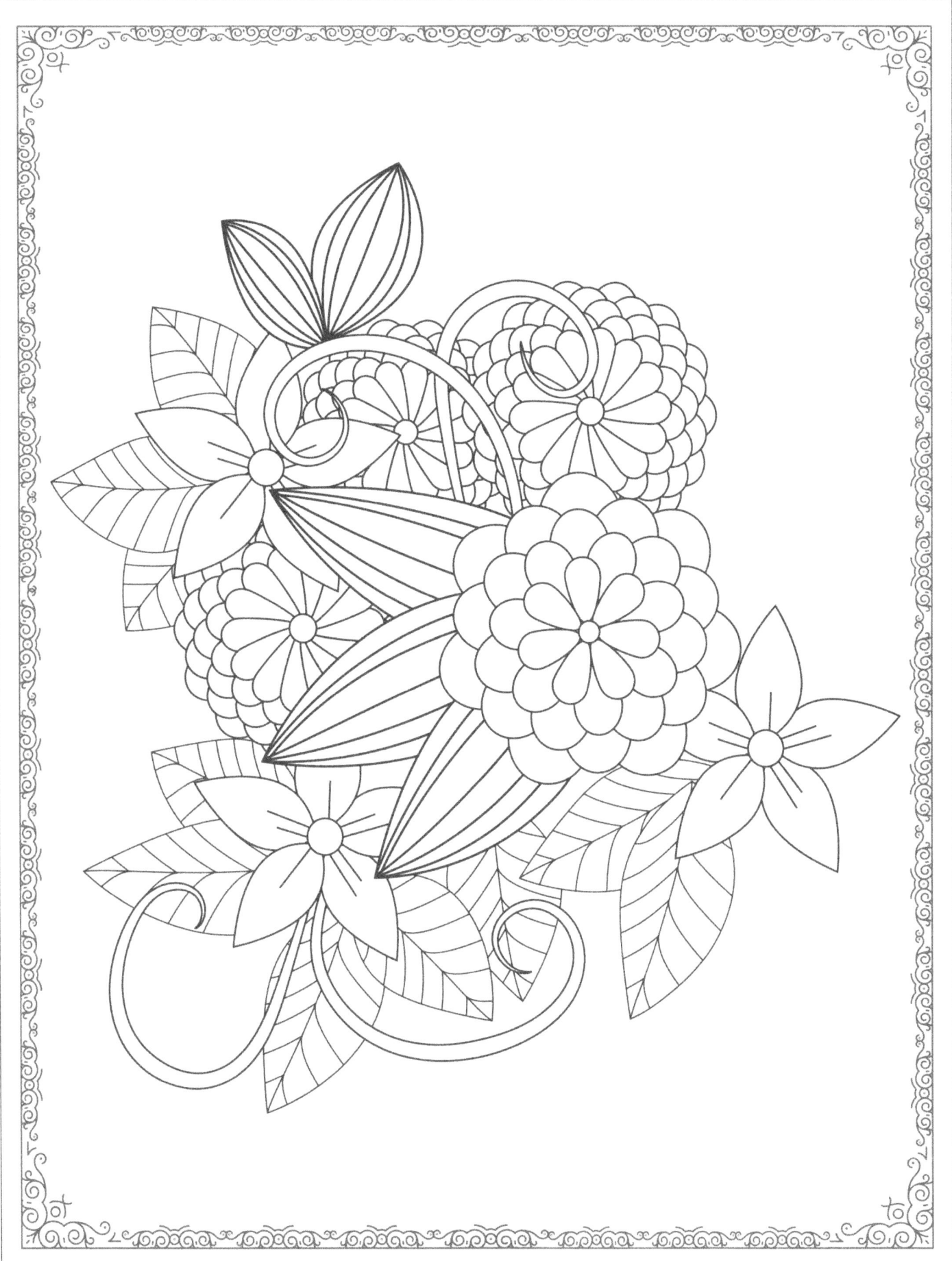

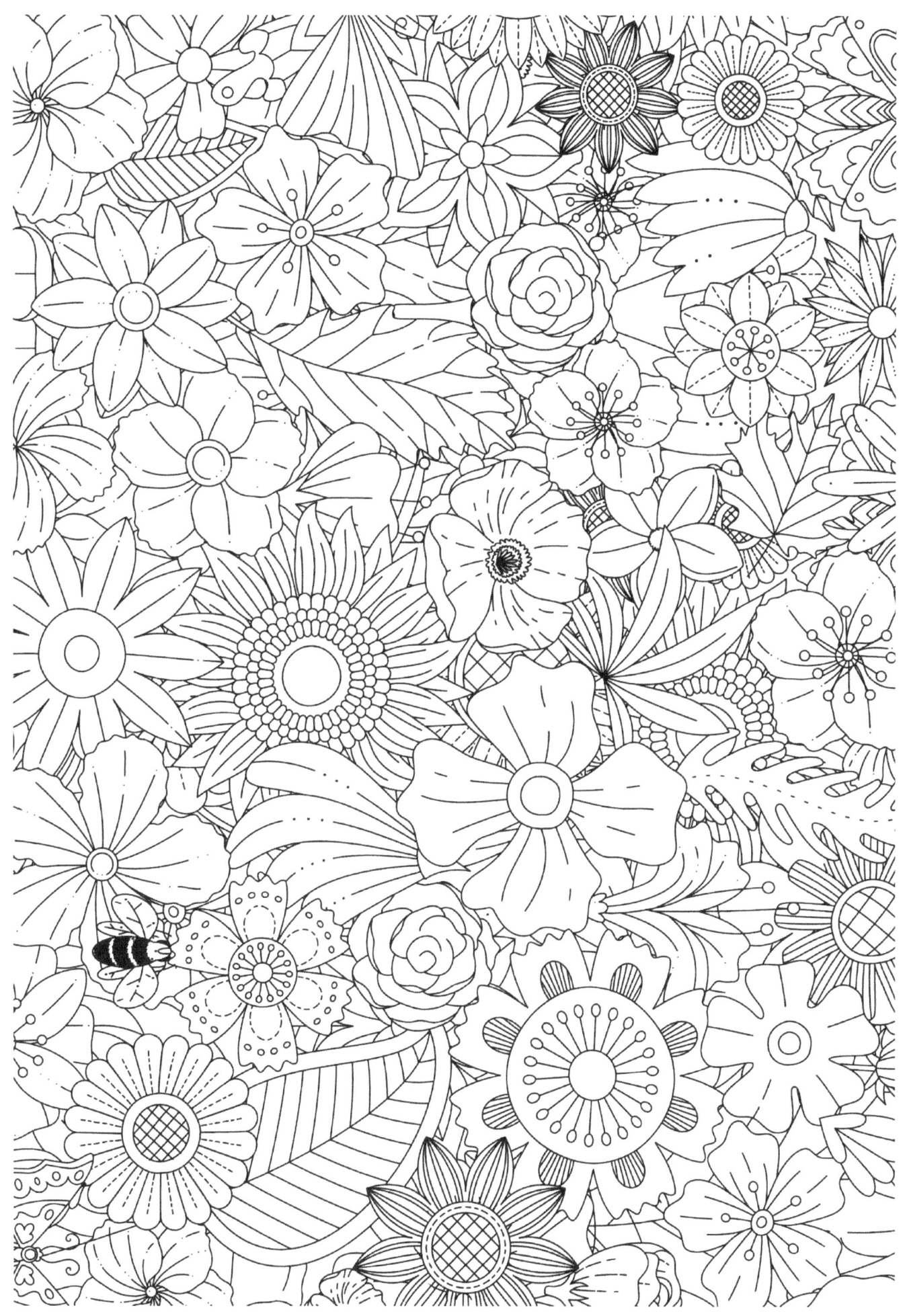

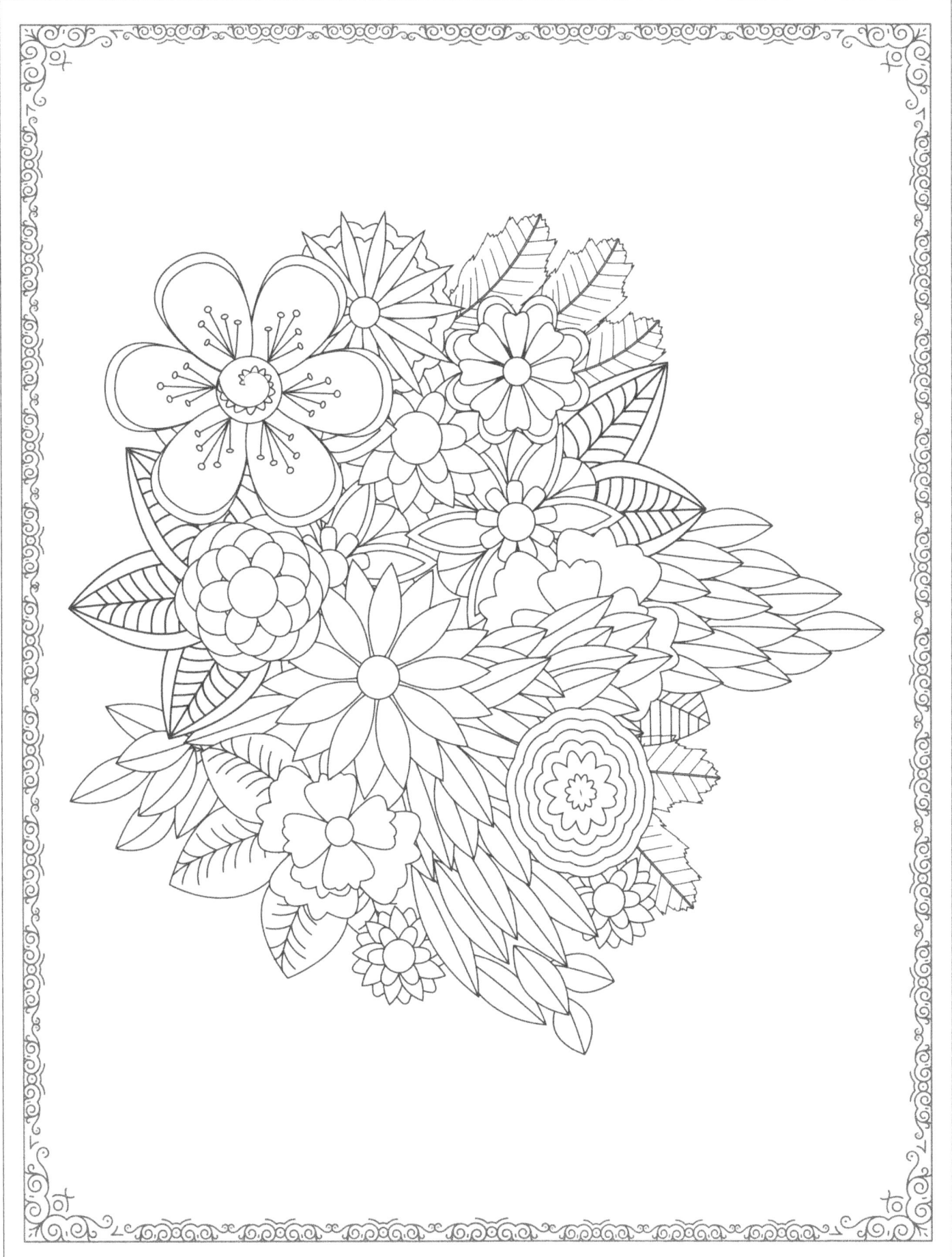

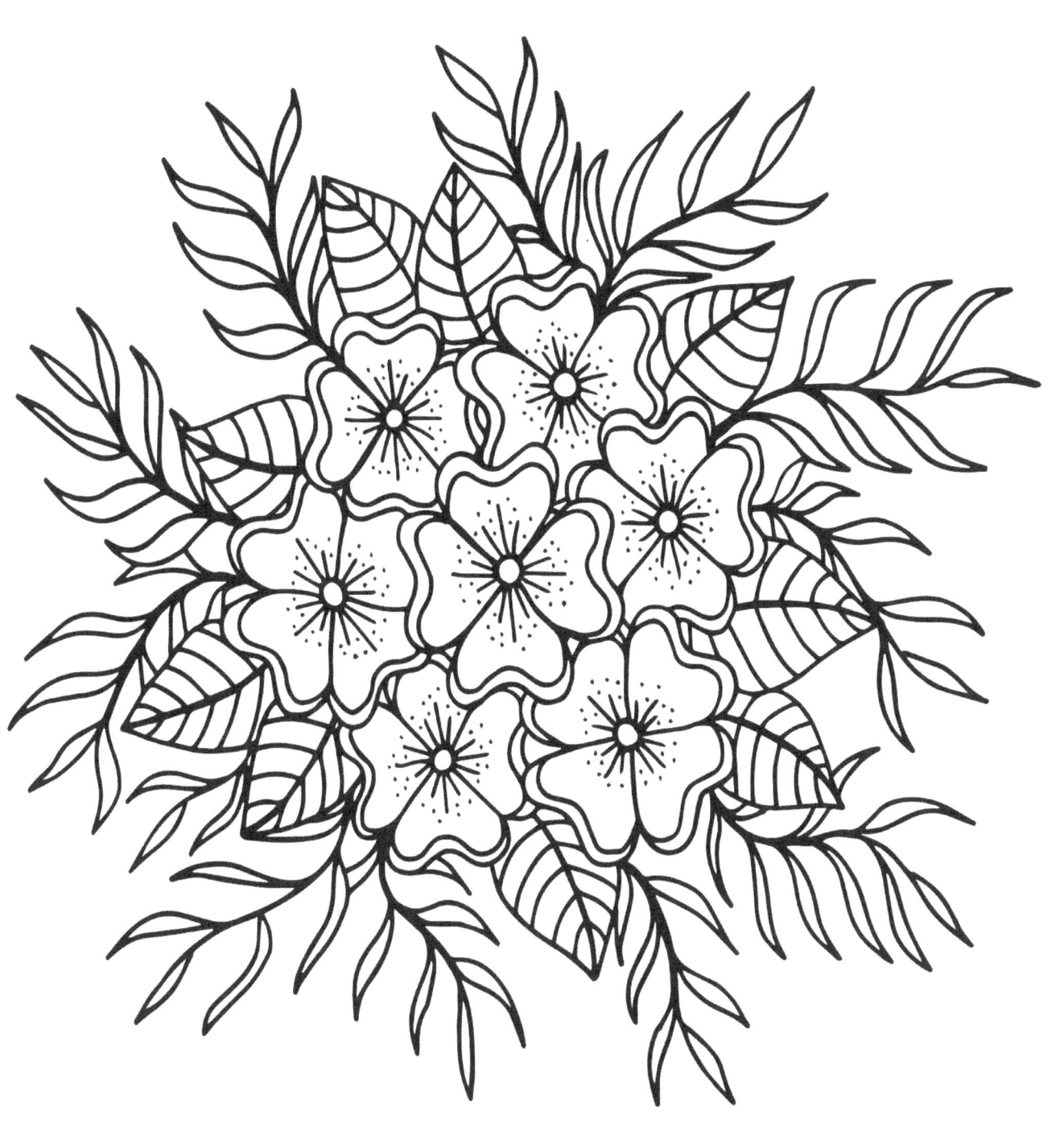

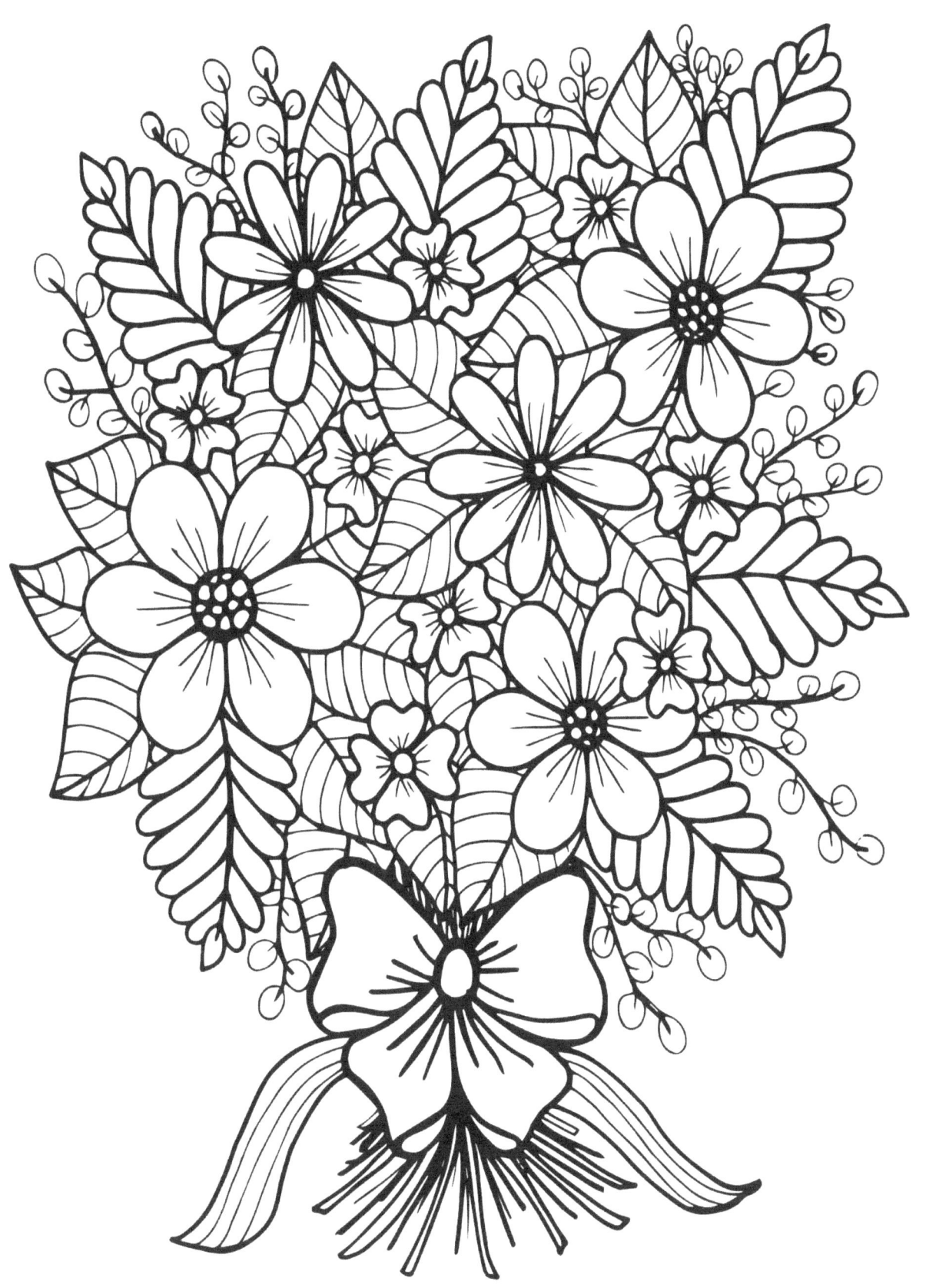

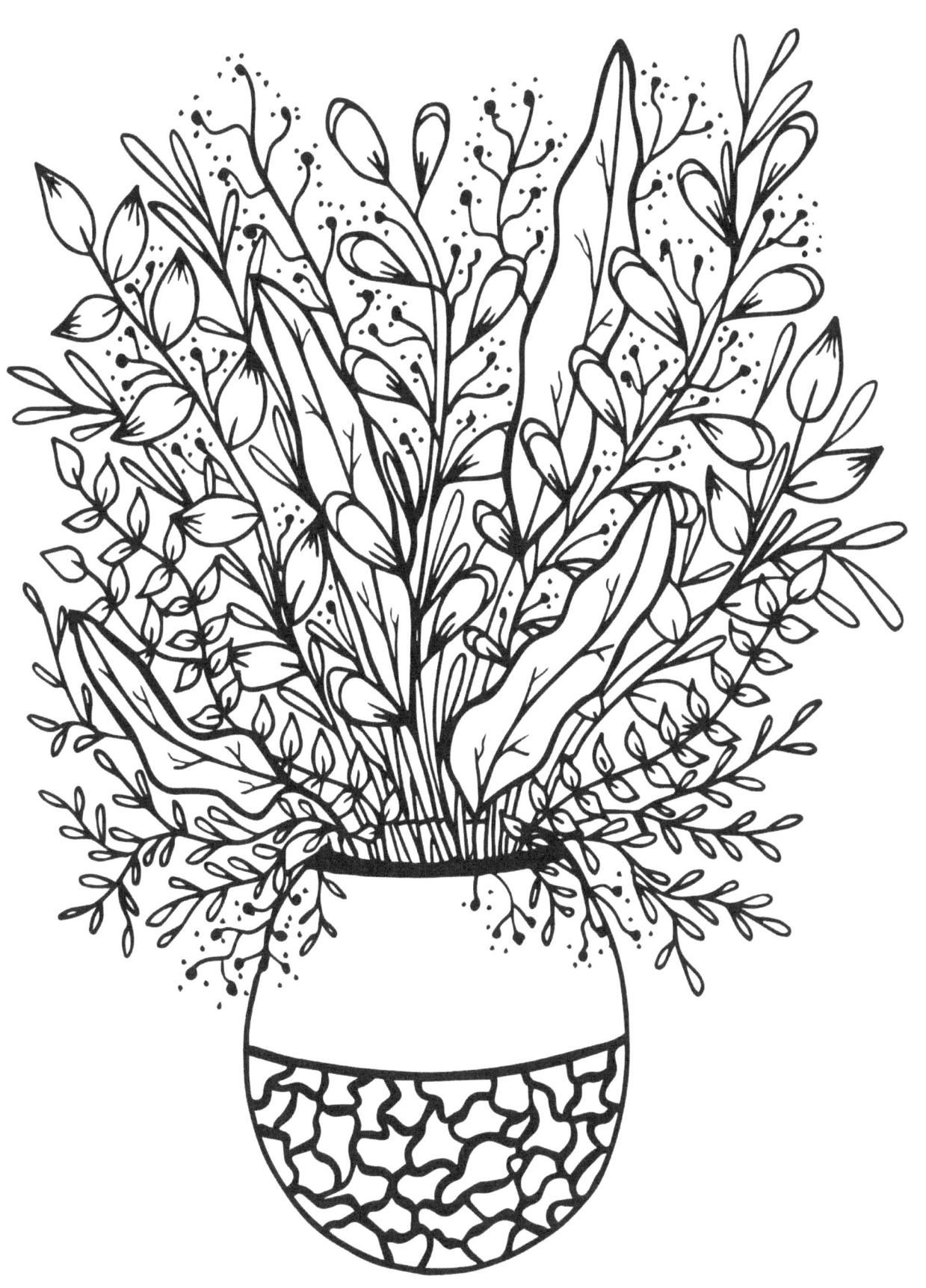

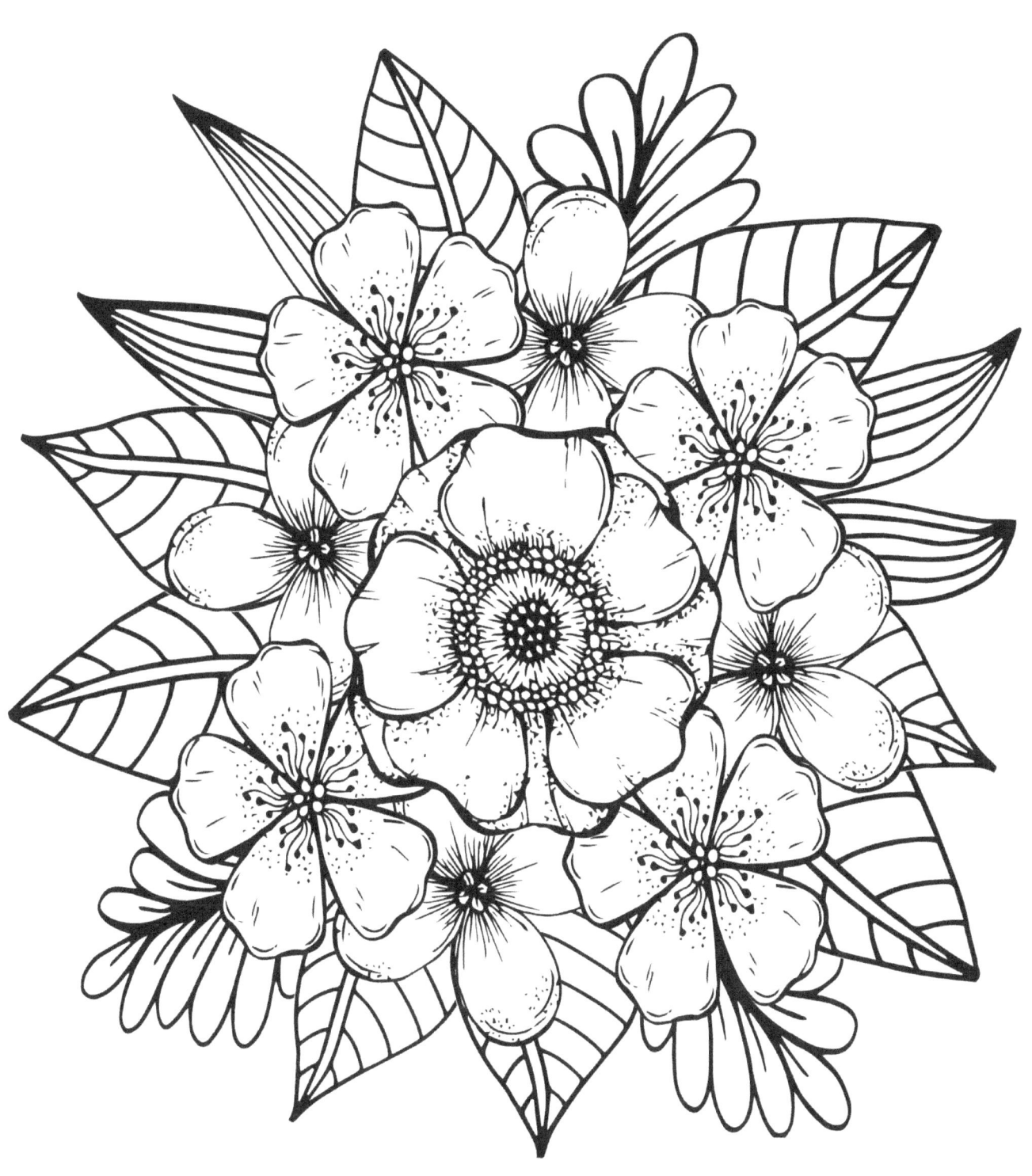

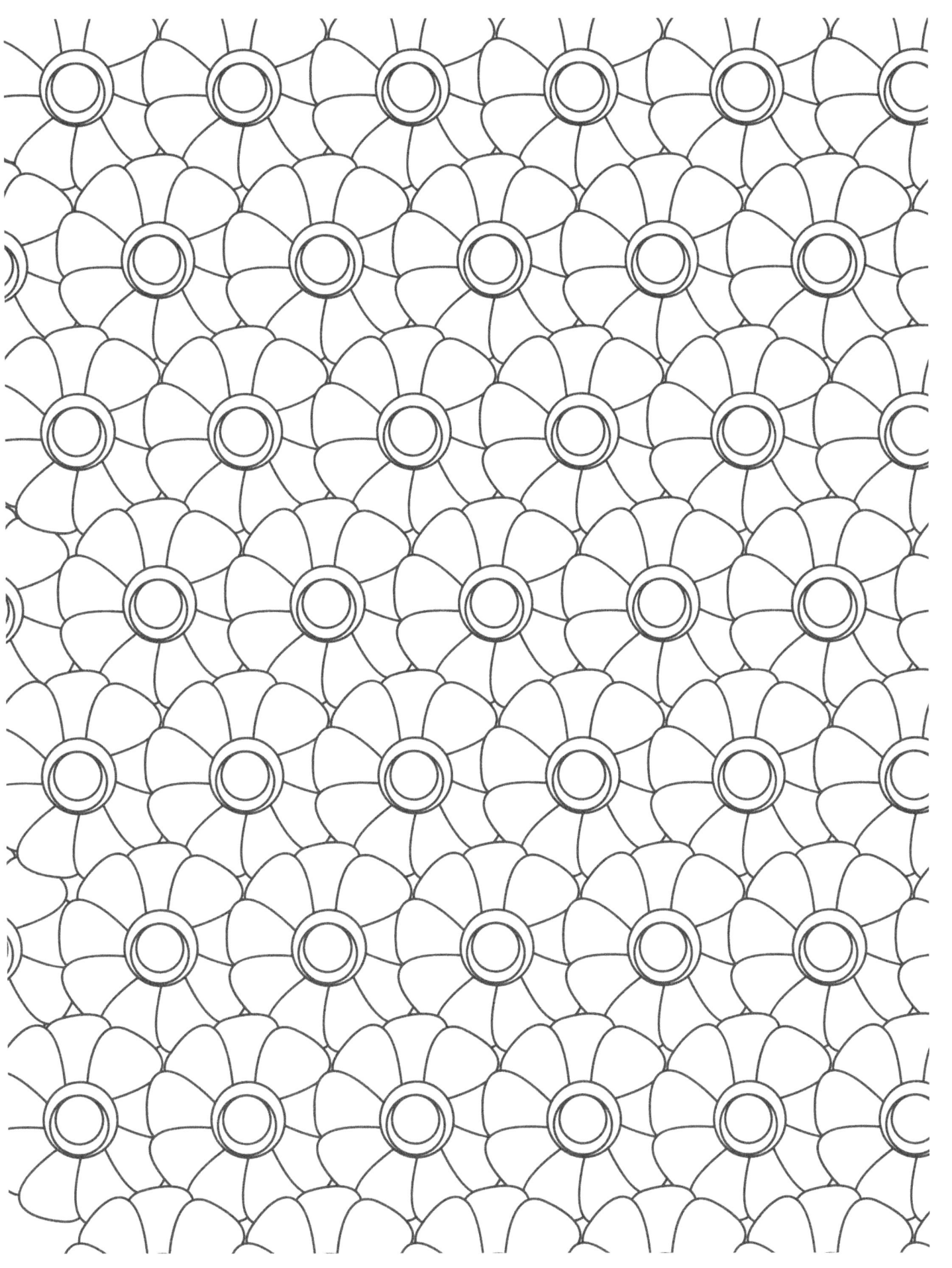

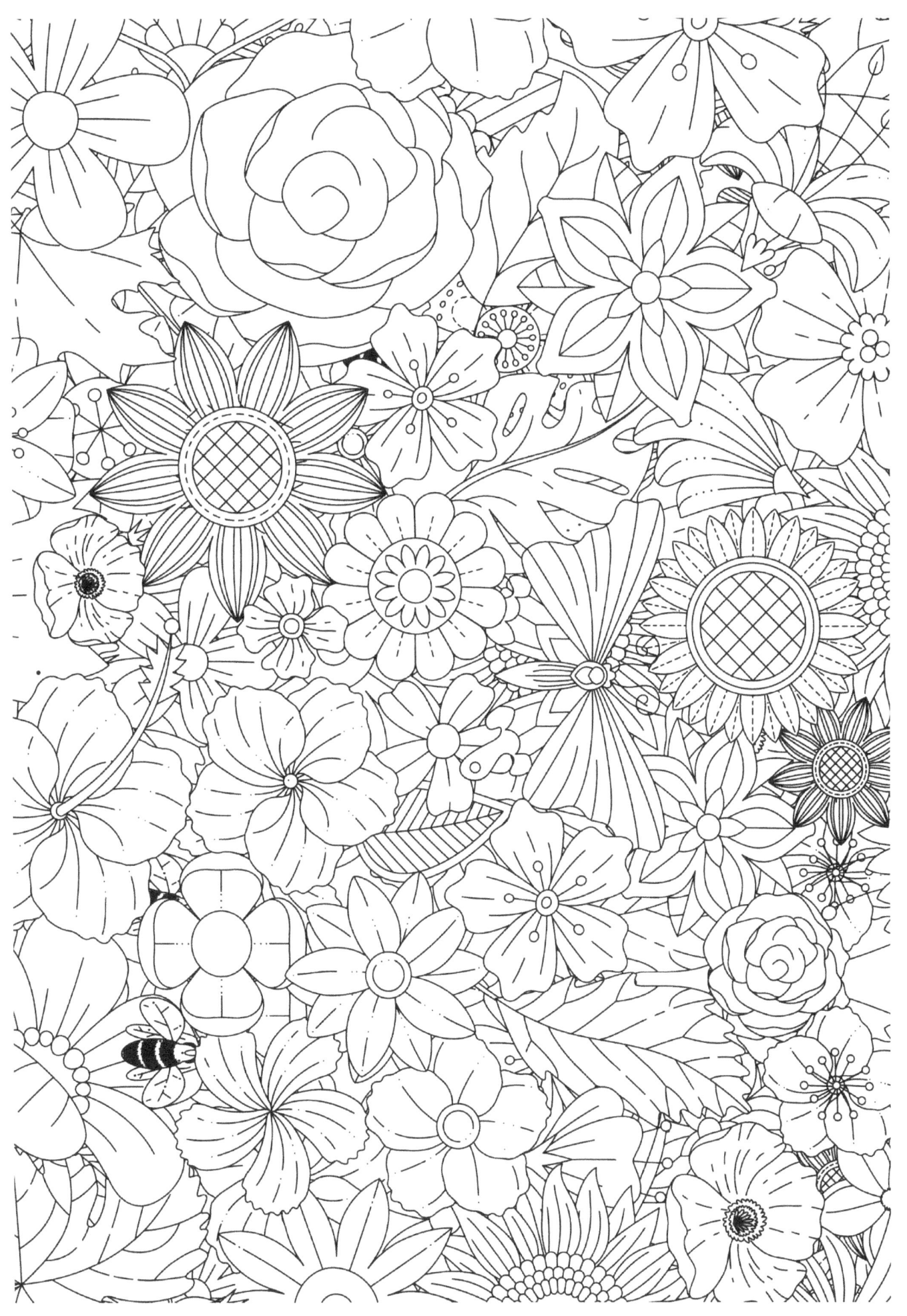

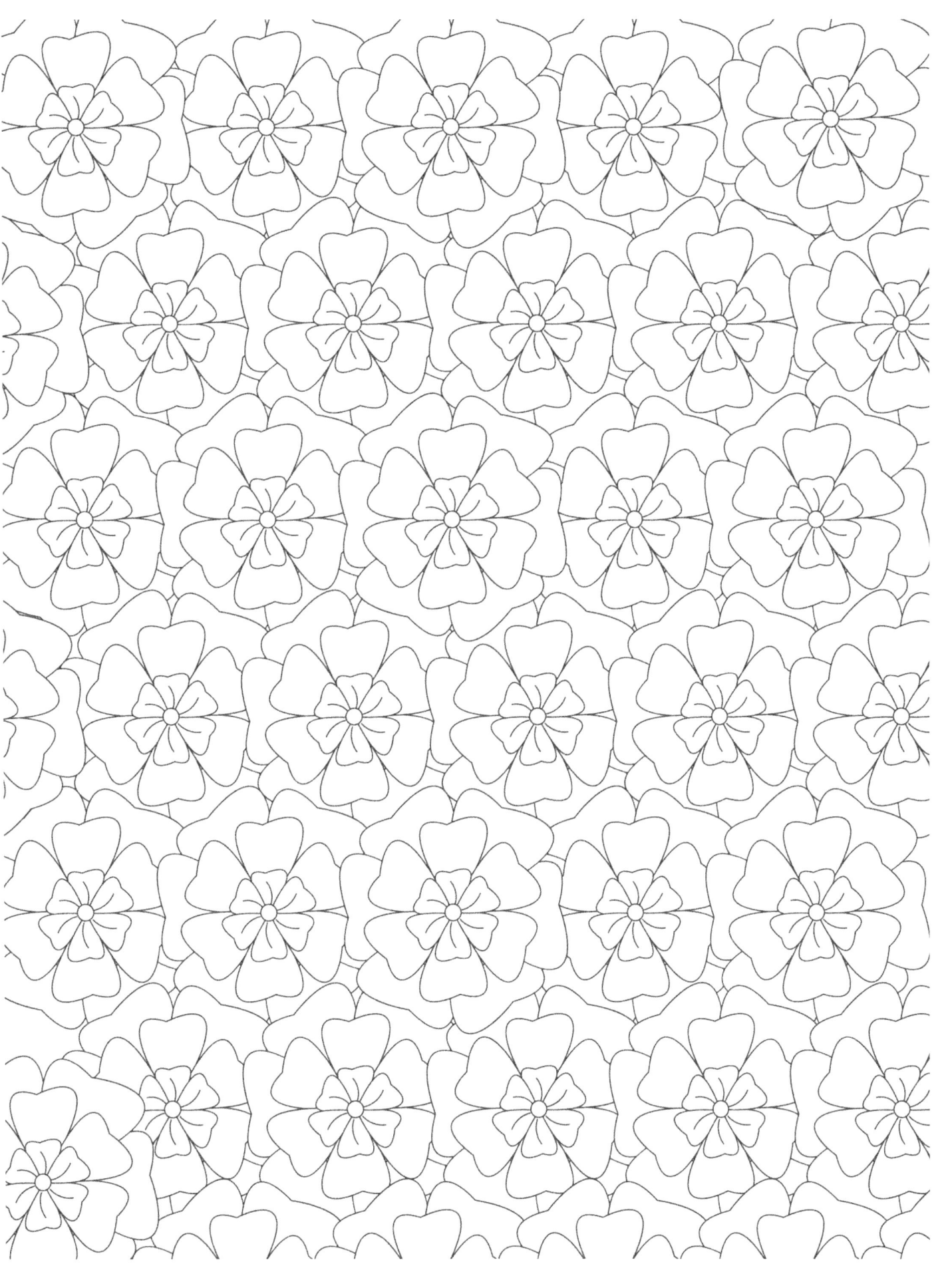

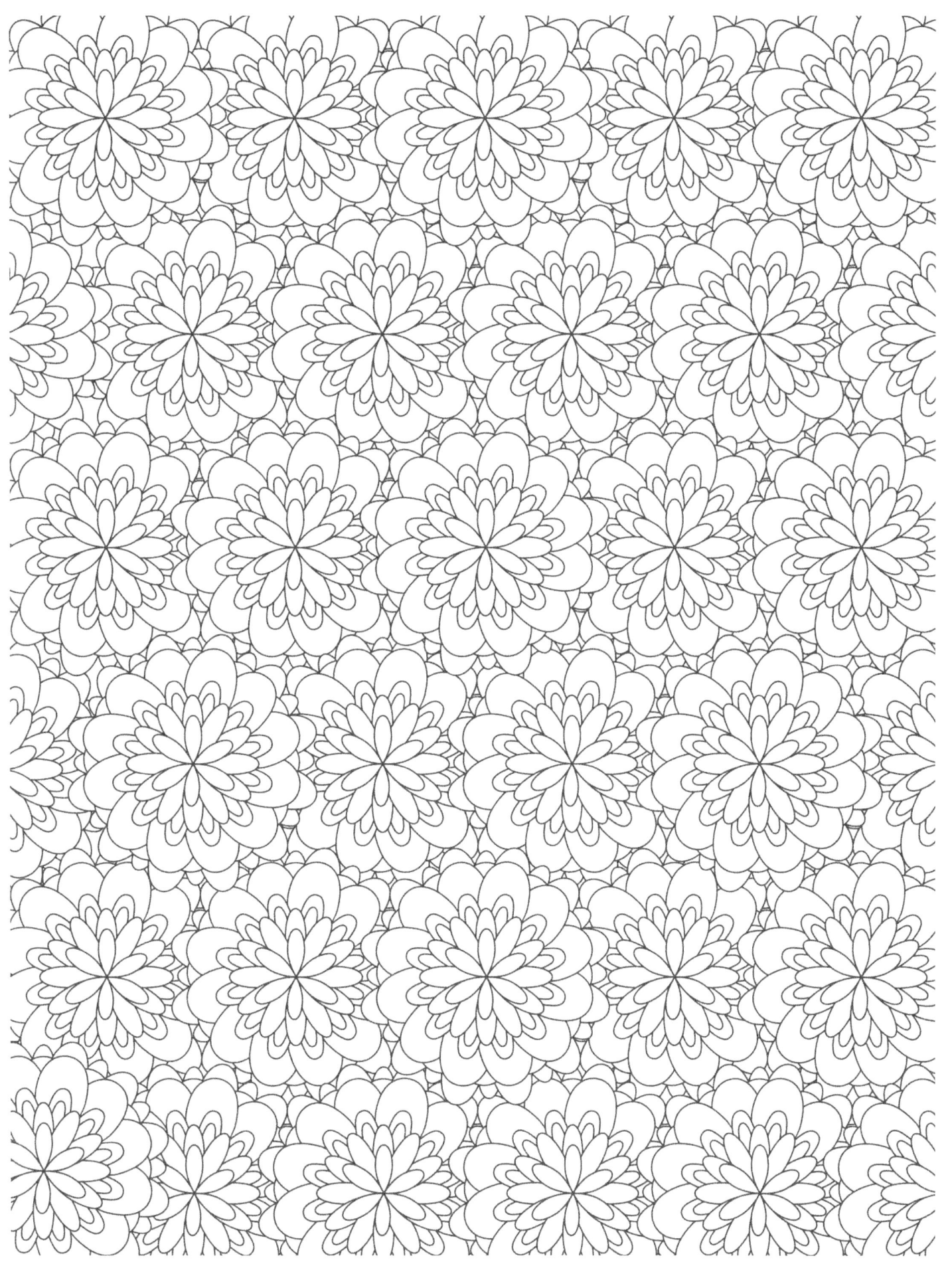

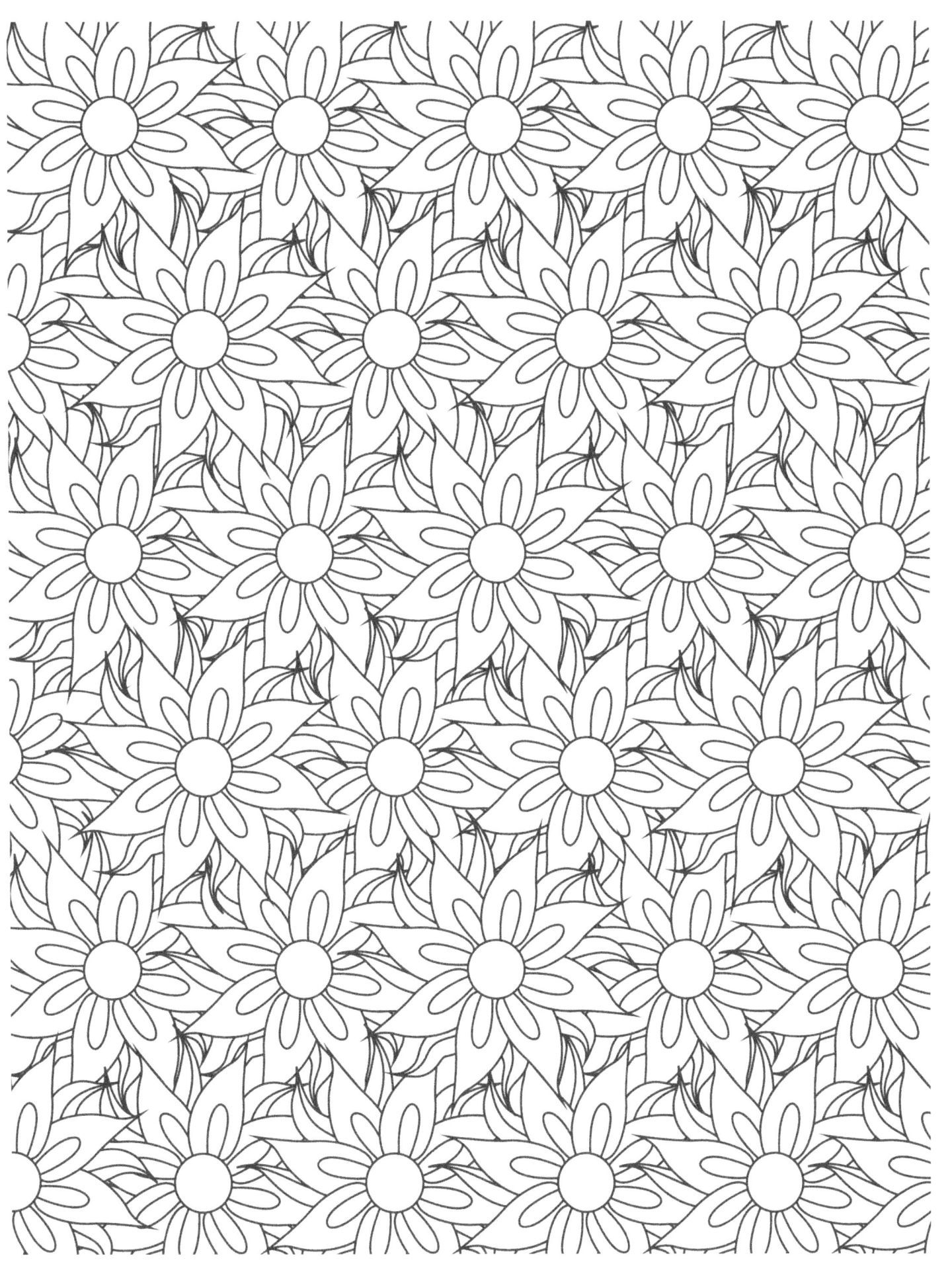

www.ingramcontent.com/pod-product-compliance
Lightning Source LLC
Chambersburg PA
CBHW081608200526
45169CB00021B/2466